Music and Religion

OXFORD THEORY IN ETHNOMUSICOLOGY

Martin Clayton, Series Editor
Martin Stokes, Series Editor

Music Theory in Ethnomusicology
Stephen Blum

Music and Citizenship
Martin Stokes

Music and Religion
Jeffers Engelhardt

Music and Religion

JEFFERS ENGELHARDT

OXFORD
UNIVERSITY PRESS

OXFORD
UNIVERSITY PRESS

Oxford University Press is a department of the University of Oxford. It furthers the University's objective of excellence in research, scholarship, and education by publishing worldwide. Oxford is a registered trade mark of Oxford University Press in the UK and in certain other countries.

Published in the United States of America by Oxford University Press
198 Madison Avenue, New York, NY 10016, United States of America.

CIP data is on file at the Library of Congress

ISBN 9780190699147 (hbk.)
ISBN 9780190699154 (pbk.)

DOI: 10.1093/9780190699185.001.0001

Paperback printed by Marquis Book Printing, Canada
Hardback printed by Lightning Source, Inc., United States of America

The manufacturer's authorized representative in the EU for product safety is Oxford University Press España S.A. of Parque Empresarial San Fernando de Henares, Avenida de Castilla, 2 – 28830 Madrid (www.oup.es/en or product.safety@oup.com). OUP España S.A. also acts as importer into Spain of products made by the manufacturer.

MIX
Paper | Supporting responsible forestry
FSC® C103567
FSC
www.fsc.org

For Triin

Epigraphs

The layman as well as the scientist would like to know how this gourd sheathed in beads and snake vertebrae, and sometimes containing a human bone, came to be the fixed and honored object that it is. It has its commandments as the voice of the gods and certainly it is hallowed. How did it get that way? Who began it? Where exactly?

—Zora Neale Hurston (1938)

If a listener from a community of believers feels blessed by the extraordinary beauty of the song and his emotional reaction to it, he may worry about the source of his pleasure: Is it the Holy Spirit or the consummate skill of the very human musician?

—Judith Becker (2004)

Because what if the whole God idea is about not-knowing and the limits of knowing, just as much as it is about knowing? Or, paradoxically, is it always both? What if, as a Sufi interlocutor of mine in Cairo says, it is about singing to God, not talking about God?

—Amira Mittermaier (2021)

Contents

List of Figures xi
Acknowledgments xiii
Prologue: Ethnomusicology, Secularity, Agency xv

Introduction: Religion's Audibility 1

1. Disentangling Religion 32

2. Entangling Religion 68

Conclusion: Religion's Inaudibility 96

Bibliography 109
Index 127

Figures

I.1 Martha leads the praise-singing session at the Mt. Calvary Holy Church Christian Restoration Centre. Video still by the author. 3

I.2 Mother and child participating in the singing at the Mt. Calvary Holy Church Christian Restoration Centre. Video still by the author. 4

1.1 *Tableau des principales religions du monde*, frontispiece from Bernard and Picart's *Cérémonies et coutumes religieuses de tous les peuples du monde*, volume 1 (1727). (© The Trustees of the British Museum 1895,1015.87.) 33

1.2 David McAllester's graphic representations (1954: 31–32) of characteristic sway song melodic profiles. (Peabody Museum Publications, Peabody Museum of Archaeology & Ethnology, Harvard University.) 39

1.3 Lois Ibsen al Faruqi's (1985: 8) hierarchy of "sound art expressions" (*handasah al-ṣawt*). (© The University of Texas Press. Reproduced with permission.) 56

1.4 Regula Burckhardt Qureshi's transcription (1995: 169) of performer/listener micro-interactions in a section of "Tōrī sūrat ke balhārī." (© Cambridge University Press. Reproduced with permission of The Licensor through PLSclear.) 60

2.1 Judith Becker's sonic-neurobiological representation (2004: 143) of the encounter between Rangda and her attackers. A trancer's core consciousness is "musicked" by Rangda's gamelan music. (© Judith Becker. Reproduced with permission.) 79

2.2 Braxton Shelley's transcription (2021: 48) of Smallwood's interpolation of Isaiah 53:3 over the hook of "Healing." 89

C.1 The Campbell Brothers—Chuck, Darick, Carlton, and Phil, clockwise from upper left. (© Jim Brock. Reproduced with permission.) 98

Acknowledgments

This project has been a close companion for nearly a decade, connecting me with friends, mentors, elders, colleagues, and students in cherished relationships. *Music and Religion* was written in a season of loss, arrival, and, somehow, sustained hope. Although it came in well past its deadline, this book became better over extra years of rubbing up against the world and maturing through others' scholarship and commentary. Thank you Martin Stokes, Martin Clayton, Suzanne Ryan-Melamed, and Lauralee Yeary for your patience and support over those years. Many friends and colleagues read the manuscript at different stages, shared conversation, answered questions, and offered generous, rigorous feedback. Thank you Melvin Butler, Amy Coddington, Tomal Hossain, Maria Mendonça, Mariam Rashid, Martin Stokes, Jeff Todd Titon, Kiara Vigil, and the anonymous readers for Oxford University Press for making this book something more than I could have produced on my own.

My experiences teaching and learning with the extraordinary students at Amherst College are written into every page of *Music and Religion*. Special thanks go to two decades worth of students, guest lecturers, and visiting artists in my Sacred Sound class and to Camila Bonilla, Luana Espinoza, and Sofia Ahmed Seid, whose reading, editing, and conversations brought this project to a finish. I am also grateful to my friends and colleagues at the *Yale Journal of Music & Religion* and to all the journal's guest editors and contributors for giving me the opportunity to read so much important new work on music and religion and to grow through your understandings of the field. Thank you Philip Bohlman, Ruth HaCohen, Martin Jean, Joanna Murdoch, Markus Rathey, Suzel Ana Reily, and Nicholas Smolenski at the *YJMR*.

I am honored that Judith Becker, Jim Brock, and Amira Mittermaier granted me permission to use their words and images here. I received essential support for this project from the Provost and Dean of the

Faculty's Office at Amherst College and from many colleagues at Amherst College, especially in the music department. The epigraphs in this book, used with permission, come from: Zora Neale Hurston, *Tell My Horse: Voodoo and Life in Haiti and Jamaica* (New York: Amistad, 2009 [1938]), 131; Judith Becker, *Deep Listeners: Music, Emotion, and Trancing* (Bloomington: Indiana University Press, 2004), 79; and Amira Mittermaier, "Beyond the Human Horizon," *Religion and Society: Advances in Research* 12 (2021): 27.

And where words come up short: thank you George Engelhardt and Carolyn Hardin Engelhardt for bringing the sounds of religion into my life from the very beginning. I wonder what you would think of this book. To Miira Engelhardt, Elli Engelhardt, and Triin Vallaste, thank you for your strength and compassion, your questions and curiosity, your laughter and wisdom, your music, and for making the Engellaste home the only place I ever want to be. *Te olete minu terve maailm.*

Prologue

Ethnomusicology, Secularity, Agency

Music and Religion is an audacious title. How many volumes would that encyclopedic project be, and with what aims? What single person could author it? A less audacious title would signal humbler intents and a tighter disciplinary focus. It would speak of ethnomusicological encounters with religion and musical ways of knowing gods, spirits, demons, and deities. But *Music and Religion* is useful for my purposes here, precisely because it unapologetically lays on the table two commonplace concepts in Europhone ethnomusicology whose uses can be productively and critically revisited. That, in short, is what this book is about: my assessment of ethnomusicology's past encounters with religion and intuitions about religion in its futures. Here I tell a story of ethnomusicology's secular disentangling of music and religion and its nonsecular entangling of *musicandreligion.* Ultimately, the play of disentangled and entangled ethnomusicologies I observe points to ways ethnomusicologists can continue working toward decolonial, antiracist futures, a more fulsome discipline, and scholarly practices that transform beyond ethnomusicology's purview.

Historically, to think in terms of music and religion is to encounter musical objects and practices framed by the social, legal, political, and epistemological category of religion. In Europhone ethnomusicology, music and religion are seemingly natural ways of listening to and writing about the sound of our discipline (music) in ritual performance, sacred spaces and places, and traditions of belief and spiritual practice (religion). Religion (possibly from the Latin *religare,* to bind) binds human and other-than-human beings, persons with institutions and identities, music and divine knowledge, and ethnomusicology with a secular methodology and epistemology. As I elaborate throughout this book, religion, far from being universal and infamously lacking a coherent definition,[1] is a category emerging out of the European Enlightenment and that continent's early modern sectarian conflicts. Religion is secular not in the sense of being illusory, disenchanted, irrational, or, in ideas of modernity as secularization, extinguishable. Rather, religion is secular in the sense of its categorical worldliness (the worldly time of the Latin *saeculum* in contrast to God's eternity in the Christian Church). In this vein, secularity and secularization are the worlding of religious life (e.g., cloistered Christian monastics becoming parish clergy) and knowledge (e.g., the *saeculum* as a grounding of Christian theology). And in its global/colonial iterations moving beyond Christianity, secularity produces religion as its own category, separated from modernity's non-religious or anti-religious publics, politics, and sovereign reason. Religion becomes, among other things, a category of difference to be administered, disciplined, and compared through the secular praxes of states and scholars.

Since its beginnings, ethnomusicology has danced with secularity in its encounters with religion. On the one hand, there is the discipline's secular unconscious: its humanist and culturalist sympathies or, alternatively, its orientation toward scientism. And on the other hand, there are musical and sonic relationships between human and other-than-human beings realized through praise, gifting, prayer, healing, divination, and sonic theologies. Until roughly the turn of the twenty-first century, ethnomusicology's standard practice was to disentangle, to varying degrees, the musical and sonic from religion in order to bracket off other-than-human agency and religious knowledge from an ethnomusicologist's findings. These are gestures of methodological atheism (gods, spirits, demons, and deities are not real) and agnosticism (they are unknowable on the other side of alterity) whose effects I trace in Chapter 1. Such gestures were commonplace, despite the presence of other-than-human agents in research participants' lives—relationships that ground them as persons—and, in some cases, ethnomusicologists' lives as religious practitioners and leaders.

These norms are entirely understandable within ethnomusicology's regnant institutional frameworks. To speak in broad strokes, ethnomusicology, in its postwar emergence as a field, clung tightly to the exclusive humanness of music (the "musical" ethnomusicology of style analysis, transcription, genre classification, and the like) and the scientism of ethnography (the "anthropological" ethnomusicology of functionalism, transmission, culture, and the like). The ethnomusicological real, in other words, was bound to the humanness of music and secular reason. Other-than-human agents—the audience of music, gifters of sound, movers of affect, bringers of (mis)fortune, cementers of relationship, vessels of knowledge and memory—were bracketed out of ethnomusicology.[2] In ethnomusicology's secular unconscious, other-than-human agents (and ethnomusicologists' knowledge of those agents) were not really real or were not admissible as explanations in the secular academic spaces ethnomusicology was inhabiting.[3] Gods, spirits, demons, and deities lived in the subjunctive. They were relegated to comments authored by primarily white, primarily male, properly atheist/agnostic, Europhone ethnomusicologists on research participants' explanations of sonic efficacy and other-than-human relationship. These other-than-human beings could not be extracted into the ethnomusicological literature that built a discipline and built careers.

And the stakes for building a discipline and building careers were high. The longstanding anthropological taboo against "going native" meant that, prior to turns anthropologist Barbara Tedlock (1991) locates in the 1970s and anthropology's crisis of representation, ethnography entailed dispassionate, objective participant observation rather than the relational, implicated observation of participation (including an ethnographer's participation). Yet even in the wake of the *Writing Culture* debates (Clifford and Marcus 1986), certain kinds of participation were suspect. In ethnographic disciplines, religion was (and still is, in many spaces) a different kind of difference, with religious participation (not to mention conversion) and references to theology straining the boundaries of those disciplines' secularity and calling into question their legitimacy in secular epistemes.

This owes, in part, to the particular Protestant Christian ethos of many secularisms in which belief and faith (rather than knowledge and practice) are the grounds of religion. An ethnomusicology grounded in religion-as-belief and religion-as-faith risked being labeled unreliable, or worse. Taking religion seriously entailed significant professional risk on the part of individual ethnomusicologists, to the detriment of the field. Contrast this situation with insider ethnographies of non-religious musicking—Paul Berliner's *Thinking in Jazz: The Infinite Art of Improvisation* (1994), for instance—in which secular knowledge of practice and experience is not only reliable, but lauded.[4] So in light of (1) the secular bias against religion-as-belief and religion-as-faith; (2) the unreason of intangible, invisible (but inaudible?) other-than-human beings; and (3) the lingering effects of anthropology's classic "rationality debates" over magic and witchcraft, ethnomusicologists sought refuge in the agnostic methods and epistemologies of comparative religion and religious studies into the 1990s. This was ethnomusicology legitimizing itself by disentangling music and religion.

Ethnomusicology's dance with secularity feels altogether different in its entangling of music and religion in the twenty-first century. In Chapter 2, I attend to the recent resurgence of nonsecular ethnomusicology that reintroduces ways of knowing about music and religion from sacred musicologies, sonic theologies, and non-Eurological traditions that secular ethnomusicology had lost connection with, or disavowed. The resurgence of nonsecular ethnomusicology comes from a number of different directions, beginning with the recognition of ethnomusicologists whose positionalities and religious lives braid together in their scholarship. Put strongly, these are ethnomusicologists who refuse to perform the secular gestures of disentangling music and religion that ethnomusicology's gatekeepers once required. An entangled ethnomusicology, therefore, becomes synonymous with a decolonial, antiracist ethnomusicological praxis: it does not eclipse disentangled approaches, but it opens the field to a more fulsome future.

Entangled ethnomusicologies are theistic (or, as I describe my earlier work, theistic-curious). By this, I mean they encounter the other-than-human agency of gods, spirits, demons, and deities as real and incorporate theology in their ethnomusicological knowing. In an entangled ethnomusicology, the effects of other-than-human agency in research participants' worlds and practices are not reduced to a functionalist warrant for human action or bracketed off as epiphenomena or unknowable—secular critique by another name. Nor is ethnomusicologists' knowledge of other-than-human agency and relationship inadmissible in their scholarship. Rather, by recognizing the entanglements of music and religion, this nonsecular mode makes strange the secular reification of music and religion as discrete, purified (Latour 1993) categories.

In this sense, an entangled ethnomusicology is at home in contemporary reassessments of secularity's politics and limits. These range from voices provincializing secularity as a mode of knowledge and social imagination[5] to the sweeping implications of anthropology's ontological turn on secular, culturalist thought.[6] A secular approach whose purview is limited to the human and the musically audible is no longer the sole ethnomusicology of religion because, in a decolonial frame, that approach is one in a pluriverse of methods and ways of knowing. Through our relationships and positionalities, music may be what we think it is, or not (Bohlman 1999), and the same holds true for the ontologies of other-than-human beings. For ethnomusicologists and religious practitioners alike, musical knowledge and knowledge of other-than-human agency can be the same thing.[7] To put it more strongly, sound (and inaudible unsound) can be media of other-than-human presence and knowledge, the grounds of human being and becoming. A story that emerges through the entanglements of *musicandreligion*, then, is that while secularity does not have an exclusive purchase on Geertz's "really real" (1966), the real of the nonsecular is also a limit of human knowing. As I propose in this book's conclusion, the audible/inaudible continuum becomes a principal space for ethnomusicological encounters with (and interventions in) religion. Along the audible/inaudible continuum, sonic knowledge of other-than-human agency and the relationships of human and other-than-human beings can become sonic humility in the presence of the more-than-human inaudible.[8]

Arrivals

I arrived at writing this book through different moments of unbelonging in my life as an ethnomusicologist—moments I have come to value abundantly upon reflection. My moments of unbelonging arrived when the default secularity of the ethnomusicological tradition I inhabit and ethnomusicology's muted suspicions of religious knowledge were bracketed off (or altogether unknown). These moments were inversions of the postwar methodological atheism and agnosticism that bracketed off questions concerning the reality of other-than-human beings. To be sure, these kinds of moments are commonplace in doing musical ethnographies of religion.

My unbelonging in ethnographic work in Orthodox Christian communities in Estonia, Greece, Romania, Russia, and the United States (sometimes as a product of my imagination and insecurities, sometimes as an explicit exclusion from spaces and communities because I am not Orthodox) is, as I remind my students, both a way into and a limit on ethnographic knowledge. Being unwelcome to enter churches and monasteries, venerate icons, sing, share meals, speak with clergy and laity, or photograph/record services has, in retrospect, been a benefit to knowing the inaudible powers of Orthodoxy. The differences that have shaped my experiences of unbelonging articulate the religious, musical, and social values of a community (I am thinking here along the lines of classic anthropological categories like purity, contamination, secrecy, and ritual failure). Moreover, they trouble the entitled assumption that all knowledge should be accessible and extractable through ethnography.[9] Ethnomusicology can do more to recognize refusal in navigating its disciplinary identity and crises (Robinson 2020).

I remember a 2006 visit to a Roma/Estonian Pentecostal congregation in the southern Estonian town of Võru to learn about their spiritual, musical, and financial links with Nordic and North American Pentecostal congregations (materialized that week in the gift of a digital synthesizer from Sweden). Midway through a service, the pastor called on me to offer testimony to the Holy Spirit's movement in my life, and I was unable to. My unbelonging—an inability to recognize, feel, hear, and attest to the Holy Spirit in my life—instantly and uncomfortably deflated the worship atmosphere and articulated a fundamental limit to the kind of knowledge I might have encountered in Võru.[10]

To be clear, this was not a limit on the gracious hospitality I received in Võru, nor was it a gesture of refusal by the Pentecostal congregation. Rather, my inability to offer testimony exposed a breach that was more absolute than a lack of musical or linguistic competence.

I suspect the tone of my refusal to offer testimony indicated to the pastor that none would be forthcoming in the future as well. I could not convert my casual Protestant commitments from home and the pull I feel from Orthodox Christian theological and artistic traditions into experiences of sonic affect, what I would call grace or mercy, and ethical personhood attributable to the Holy Spirit's agency and in Pentecostal terms. Moreover, because my initial visit ended up being a one-off visit, I did not invest enough in the Võru congregation to learn their theological language, ways of worshipping, and how I might offer some form of sincere testimony. In contrast to the years of investment I made in Orthodox Christian communities in Estonia, which taught me theological language, opened me to the knowledge of practice, and made me feel ready to publish ethnographic work (Engelhardt 2015), my experience in Võru was of a secular ethnomusicology's abject shortcomings. There, my abilities to move beyond music's audible envelope toward the sounded relationships of human and other-than-human beings were scant. I could feel myself defaulting to an ethnomusicology that disentangled music and religion in order to render the former knowable and the latter a culturalist form of difference. I tabled the nascent project.

In my life as a scholar and teacher, other spaces of unbelonging have been equally as formative. Over the past two decades, sharing work and encountering others' research in nonsecular academic spaces has helped me reassess the privileging of secular ethnomusicology in my life and career. Although it may seem odd to frame my association with the Yale Institute of Sacred Music (visiting faculty) and the *Yale Journal of Music & Religion* (editor-in-chief since 2016) as unbelonging, the unremarkable intermixing of secular and nonsecular approaches to music studies I have encountered in that work has productively thrown into relief the ideological surroundings of my life as a scholar and teacher. The Yale Institute of Sacred Music is an unusual space where theologically informed approaches to religious arts and their applications are in close dialogue with secular scholarly traditions, and the scholarship submitted to the *Yale Journal of Music & Religion* is often written beyond the Eurological traditions of secular music studies. In attending to the frictions and difference I have felt in those encounters, I have gained increasing clarity on the stakes of disentangled and entangled ethnomusicologies. Elsewhere, beyond my English-dominant comfort zones of Society for Ethnomusicology, American Musicological Society, British Forum for Ethnomusicology, and International Council for Traditions of Music and Dance conferences, where to speak the language of secular critique (Asad et al. 2009) is to belong, time spent at International Society for Orthodox Church Music, Christian Congregational Music, and Saint Vladimir's Orthodox Theological Seminary conferences, among others, has, through my sense of unbelonging, accented the critical potentials of nonsecular ethnomusicologies.

Those potentials share much in common with ethnomusicology's hoped-for, decolonial, antiracist futures.[11] Collaborating with clergy, theologians, and scholars whose epistemologies incorporate divine mystery, who use scripture and the words of saints as theory and evidence, and who sing and listen to sound as sacred gifts has humbled the prestige of the secular ethnomusicology I was taught to leverage.[12] And at the same time, the aporias of nonsecular approaches are comparable to secular ones—positionality and praxis by other names. My point here is that as the entanglements of music and religion become more commonplace in ethnomusicology (see Chapter 2) and are recognized alongside the field's usual disentangling of music and religion (see Chapter 1), ethnomusicologists previously excluded from the discipline's canons and career pathways receive recognition and opportunities. This is what I mean when I write of ethnomusicology's more fulsome futures. To be clear, however, I am not suggesting a chronological hierarchy with ethnomusicology's secular, disentangling pastness as less than its nonsecular, entangling future.[13] As I elaborate in this book's conclusion, (dis)entangled ethnomusicologies commingle in the field's current moment, and that is a good thing for ethnomusicology to transform itself in addressing the challenges and honoring the traditions of its secular, human-centered, culturalist legacies.

Music and Religion is an exercise in putting those significant terms into fruitful proximity. It is a story about ethnomusicologists using those readymade categories productively, and resisting them; a story about ethnomusicologists reasoning with other-than-human agency by bracketing it off and relating to other-than-human agency through onto-epistemic difference; a story about ethnomusicology's history of disentangling and entangling music and religion. This book is an invitation to re-read and re-hear some of ethnomusicology's canons and discern ethnomusicology's promise for understanding relationships of human and other-than-human beings in a moment of planetary precarity. It is also offered as sustenance, perhaps, for those who, like me, experience ethnomusicology as something akin to a spiritual discipline[14] that can attune and expose us to other-than-human presences in our worlds.

Notes

1. For religious studies scholar Andrew Dole, religion's "vagueness" makes determining whether a phenomenon is religious, defining constituent elements of a religion, and locating boundaries between religions unachievable (2024: 758). On "Religion before the Academy," see Halverson 2024.
2. An interesting parallel can be found in German colonial linguistics and the sound recording of African prisoners of war in German camps during World War I. As Anette Hoffmann explains, Yevegbe is "a widely known lingual practice [among Ewe speakers] by means of which gods spoke (or speak) through a possessed person to communicate with their followers" (2024: 127). However, "because the possibility of embodying a speaking deity did not occur to the linguists," Hoffman writes, "they heard [Stephan] Bischoff [interned as a British subject from the Gold Coast] sing in a feigned voice. Yet, when asked for the Lautarchiv records which languages he spoke, Bischoff did not mention Yevegbe. He did not mention it because he did not actively speak this language. By means of his drumming he summoned the deity. On recording PK 863/3, one hears So [a deity] speaking through Bischoff" (2024: 128).
3. Religious historian Robert Orsi reserves some of his sharpest critique for this contradiction in the secular academy: "The liberal secular university [. . .] is the site of manifold prohibitions masquerading as permissions. Liberal piety opens the space for anything to be studied critically as long as the critical perspective brought into play is not religiously particular, and thus theology, which is always particularist, has been exiled by academic liberalism" (2005: 193). On the resurgence of theology-as-theory in ethnographic disciplines, see Chapter 2.
4. I am grateful to Jeff Todd Titon for this comparative observation.
5. Now-classic examples include Talal Asad's *Formations of the Secular: Christianity, Islam, Modernity* (2003), Dipesh Chakrabarty's *Provincializing Europe: Postcolonial Thought and Historical Difference* (2000), Saba Mahmood's *Politics of Piety: The Islamic Revival and the Feminist Subject* (2005), Charles Taylor's *A Secular Age* (2007), and Peter van der Veer's *The Modern Spirit of Asia: The Spiritual and Secular in China and India* (2014).
6. In broad strokes, I am thinking here of work that reminds us how the existence of things and persons (including nonhuman persons) in their worlds is radically relative. Absent a natural essence (the supposed foil of cultural difference), objects and beings exist in being known, the ontological and the epistemological dissolving into the other. See Bennett (2010), Bessire and Bond (2014), Descola (2013), Graeber (2015), Ochoa Gautier (2014), Pickering (2017), and Viveiros de Castro (1998).

7. Here I am echoing Yahya Jongintaba's (formerly known as Jon Michael Spencer) call for a practice of theomusicology (Spencer 1991), but as a mode of contemporary ethnomusicology rather than a separate discipline.
8. This point about other-than-human agency, human/other-than-human relationship, and the more-than-human inaudible is not, of course, limited to religion—a fact that accentuates the limits of religion's categorical enclosure. Put differently, an other-than-human turn in ethnomusicology can recast the relationship of music and religion without being about religion itself. Charles Taylor says something similar with regard to Romantic aesthetics: "If the gods without us cannot feel, then presumably they cannot act either. Our feelings of joyful response to their action are not only a condition of our *awareness* of this beneficent intervention in our lives, but more radically, of this intervention itself, of there being divine *agents* at all" (2024: 99).
9. I am thinking here of how the two "r-words" (research and refusal) (Tuck and Yang 2014) intersect in ethnomusicology's decolonial efforts, including those along former Cold War global binaries (Engelhardt and Pukinskis 2024; Tlostanova 2023).
10. This is, of course, the most common of ethnographic impasses, and it is not limited to religion. In my view, however, the religious version of this impasse stands out in secular academic spaces. Relative to other registers of difference, which are commonly framed as potentially generative in ethnography, the religious us/them impasse amounts to a taboo in secular ethnomusicology (see Chapter 1). In Chapter 2, I account for a recent "season of experimenting with ways of rethinking this great boundary" (Orsi 2005: 175) in nonsecular ethnomusicologies.
11. In *The Coloniality of the Secular*, religious studies scholar An Yountae renews our attention to the connections of religious/nonsecular critique and the decolonial. "We witness religion's broad implication in the world not only as a system of power that sanctions violence," An writes, "but also as the driving motor behind counterhegemonic forces that seek to build a new order" (2024: 2). While An is in conversation primarily with Africana critical theorists, his thinking translates, imperfectly but powerfully, into other decolonial worlds, including the "post-post-Soviet" spaces in which I work.
12. These collaborations include my coeditors and many contributors to *Arvo Pärt: Sounding the Sacred* (Bouteneff, Engelhardt, and Saler 2021), *Studying Congregational Music: Key Issues, Methods, and Theoretical Perspectives* (Mall, Engelhardt, and Ingalls 2021), and *Resounding Transcendence: Transitions in Music, Religion, and Ritual* (Engelhardt and Bohlman 2016).
13. This is a hierarchy that would invert Johannes Fabian's hierarchy of a secularized present/sacred past in the "denial of coevalness" put forth in *Time and the Other* (1983).
14. I borrow this formulation from Tanya Luhrmann's thinking on the prospects of anthropology as a spiritual discipline (2023).

Introduction

Religion's Audibility

On the afternoon of July 9, 2008, several dozen women, mostly Christian, some Muslim, and many with young children in tow, assembled at the Mt. Calvary Holy Church Christian Restoration Centre in the Kayole district of Nairobi, Kenya. They came to the church for a meeting led by the pastor, his wife, and representatives from a microfinance NGO to hear about the merry-go-round lending circles (*chama*s in Kiswahili) established there. I was at the church that day in connection with research I was doing with the NGO on musicians and microfinance participation in Nairobi.

In one of their forms, urban chamas are trust-based groups of women with limited access to credit who commit to making small monthly payments into a shared pool of capital that is loaned out serially or through consensus to help meet women's financial needs: housing repairs, rent, wedding or funeral expenses, children's school fees, or money for a vending business, for instance. Because they are informal and trust based, chamas entail risk for all involved, since someone who has received a payment could default on future contributions. To insure against this risk, transparency, obligation, and trust are performed as *chama* participants pool and distribute cash at a meeting, transforming barriers to accessing credit into a reciprocal act of social support (chamas are consonant with Christian and Muslim perspectives on usury and personal finance).

The Mt. Calvary Holy Church Christian Restoration Centre is situated along a side street in the Matopeni neighborhood of Kayole. Built on packed earth from panels of particle board, plywood, and corrugated metal around a timber frame, it is large enough to accommodate two wide aisles with six rows of white plastic chairs and wooden benches—just enough seating for the women and children who filled

Music and Religion. Jeffers Engelhardt, Oxford University Press.
 DOI: 10.1093/9780190699185.003.0001

the space that Wednesday afternoon (the church's pastor and I were the only men there). The church is lit with natural light that pours in through open windows when the turquoise wooden shutters are opened. Some of the particle board walls are painted white; some of the plywood walls are untreated. The front wall of the Mt. Calvary Holy Church Christian Restoration Centre is hung with colorful satin fabric, and a verse from Hosea (6:1) is painted beneath the arched plywood ceiling: "Come, let us return to the Lord." As women gathered in the church that afternoon, "Martha," the pastor's wife, dressed in a dark pink suit and standing opposite the podium where her husband preaches, led a praise-singing session to prepare for the meeting. Singing *mapambio*, a call-and-response style, in the ethnically/geographically neutral Kiswahili, hands clapping and interlocking at 109 beats per minute, unaccompanied voices warming up to brighter and brighter timbres, and investing more and more energy in the sound, the women began to braid their hesitancy and hopes around a God made present through praise, and each other:

MARTHA Oh Father, we lift you up, we're singing, receive praise
WOMEN Eh Father, Eh Father, Eh Father, receive the praise, receive the praise, receive the praise, receive the praise, alleluia
MARTHA Oh Father, praise belongs to you, oh praise belongs to you
WOMEN Eh Father, Eh Father, Eh Father, receive the praise
MARTHA Oh Father, praise belongs to you, oh praise belongs to you
WOMEN Eh Father, Eh Father, Eh Father, receive the praise, receive the praise, receive the praise, receive the praise, alleluia
MARTHA Father we praise you, receive the praise and glory
WOMEN [ululations]
MARTHA Yahweh, Yahweh, Yahweh, Yahweh, there is Yahweh
WOMEN Yahweh, Yahweh, Yahweh, Yahweh, Yahweh, Yahweh, there is Yahweh
MARTHA You save hearts, Yahweh, you replenish, Yahweh, there is no God like you
WOMEN Yahweh, Yahweh, Yahweh, Yahweh, Yahweh, Yahweh, there is no God like you
MARTHA We lift you, we worship you
WOMEN Yahweh, Yahweh there is no God like you

MARTHA We glorify you, we wait upon you
WOMEN Yahweh, Yahweh there is no God like you
MARTHA Yahweh, you heal us, Yahweh you care for us
WOMEN Yahweh, Yahweh there is no God like you
MARTHA Father, all glory is from you
WOMEN Father, all glory is from you
MARTHA We give all our thanks to you
WOMEN We give all our thanks to you[1]

For thirty minutes, Martha (see Figure I.1) guided an unbroken flow of call-and-response praise singing, collected[2] voices increasing in density and intensity as the singing poured out from the church into the muddy streets (Matopeni means "in the mud" in Kiswahili) lined with wattle and daub homes and cinder block shops, beckoning more and more women inside. As preparation for the meeting about chama participation, the women's singing was not only praise for God

Figure I.1 Martha leads the praise-singing session at the Mt. Calvary Holy Church Christian Restoration Centre. Video still by the author.

as Father (*baba*) and the Israelite's Yahweh, whose agency and presence are uniquely worthy of worship. The women (see Figure I.2) were also singing about their singing ("we lift you up, we're singing, receive praise"), reflexively voicing themselves in relation to God, framing risk, trust, and obligation in terms of God's past action in the world, praiseworthiness in the present, and endurance into the future. Through the qualities of quantity and mass mounting in the sound of their collected praise, these women made it possible to think of chama participation—a leap of faith into new social and financial relationships and access to credit—in terms of divine action. Not only a musical process and artifact of improvisation, mapambio praise singing socialized the presence of God's agency in the densities and intensities of the women's voices. Its possibilities were born out in ardent, tearful testimonies from chama participants following the praise-singing session that evidenced God's movement in their lives and echoed the women's praise. God, hailed as the auditor of

Figure I.2 Mother and child participating in the singing at the Mt. Calvary Holy Church Christian Restoration Centre. Video still by the author.

the women's praise, was an essential agent in their inchoate social network.

In the wake of the post-election ethnic violence and mass displacement throughout Kenya that directly affected women at the Mt. Calvary Holy Church Christian Restoration Centre in 2007–2008, the intensified forms of risk, trust, and obligation that chama participation entailed intensified the atmosphere of voices collected in praise.[3] Those voices made it possible to live through trauma and precarity wrought by violence and displacement by relating chama participation to God's past, present, and future action. This was an atmosphere at peace with some women's ambivalent commitment and their aversion to the risks and rewards of chama participation. The drawn-out moment and affective rush of interfaith, inter-ethnic praise singing that Wednesday afternoon addressed the women who could and the women who did not experience God's presence in the social support of making credit accessible in fraught times and precarious lives. In that corner of the Matopeni neighborhood, the women's singing voiced differential relationships with a god made uncontestably present.

Ethnomusicology and Religion

In my description of praise singing as preparation for chama participation at the Mt. Calvary Holy Church Christian Restoration Centre, religion is difficult to pin down—certainly more difficult to pin down than the god whose presence I theistically insist upon. Religion is difficult to think with across times and traditions on either side of its invention, which is of relatively modern vintage and dated in many stories to Catholic/Protestant conflict in seventeenth- and eighteenth-century Europe and European colonizers' encounters with religious difference.[4] Otherwise, in place of religion's "isms," we have self-definitions like *dharmavinaya* (Buddha teaching and discipline), *Sikhī* (teachings), Orthodoxy (correct belief/worship), Islam (submission to God), *Ìṣẹ̀ṣẹ* (original traditions), and so many other terms for religious systems, communities, and practices that strain against that term's enclosure.[5] Making religion (and listening and writing in terms of religion) is a secular project whose consequences echo throughout the history of ethnomusicology as a field (and music studies more broadly).[6] For my purposes in this book, religion, often used as an exogenous category, is many things, including:

- Conventional, shorthand "isms" meant to identify core doctrines, rituals, and institutions, manage heterodoxy, and differentiate religions at their nebulous boundaries and spaces of contact;
- Rituals channeling sacred power to effect a transformation of participants' worlds and their relationships with human and other-than-human beings;[7]
- Quotidian and exceptional practices of prayer, purification, pilgrimage, healing, sacrifice, storytelling, musicking, dancing, and bodily disciplining not fully described or captured by the "isms" of world religions;[8]
- Materials, objects, and technologies that mediate sensorially between humans, other-than-humans, and interworldly times and spaces;[9]
- Institutions and "authorizing discourses" (Asad 1993) invested in the reproduction of durable religious ideologies and practices;[10]
- Knowledge about cosmology and human relationships with divinities, demons, and other-than-human beings, existential doubts and fears, and experiences of transcendence, encounter, and revelation inaccessible to others;[11]
- Social identities and legal recognitions that secure forms of life set apart and sacred: congregation, *ummah*, *saṅgha*, and ethnonational or religious monocultures;[12]
- Sacrifice, gifts, and forms of difference and exchange that structure and flow through human-divine relationships, markets, and concentrations of capital;[13]
- Spaces of sanctuary and refusal in which marginalized communities become integral and sovereign.[14]

As a frame for thinking at the intersections of the sacred and the social (and, not unproblematically, doing the secular work of erecting boundaries between the two), religion can be an organizing category as intuitively natural as it is charged,[15] not unlike the frame of music in ethnomusicology and music studies.[16] Does God receive the women's sung praise at the Mt. Calvary Holy Church Christian Restoration Centre as a performative sonic offering, thereby realizing a right relationship between God and humanity, or does their singing pragmatically invoke Father/Yahweh to orient risk, trust, and obligation in relation to the absolute? Does the women's worship recognize God's real, unique power or does it create that power through human action? Does praise singing express one's readiness to participate in God's action (a merry-go-round lending circle being *of* God) or is it a means of performing one's way into a chama (vocal public piety as access to credit)? Does an other-than-human being figure into the "acoustic assemblages" (Ochoa Gautier 2014: 22) of calling, listening, and responding in praise singing, or does music remain bound to a singularly human world of sounding vibration and events? Do the sonic qualities of the women's voices index experiences of God's presence and action or are they culturally stylized channels for engaging gender ideologies?

In the story of twentieth- and twenty-first-century ethnomusicologies I relate here, the answer to all these questions, in a spirit of disrupting the secular/nonsecular binaries they construct, is yes.[17] Yes, divine, other-than-human beings and sacred objects *are* agents in the world with social and sonic relationships to humans. Yes, divine, other-than-human beings and sacred objects *become* agents in the world through the sounds and affordances of ritual practice. Yes, sacred sound, whether composed by humans or revealed to them, mediates—is in the midst of, as infrastructure—the binds between humans, the divine, and other-than-human beings. Yes, performing sacred traditions can be an expedient means of accessing or strengthening social networks. Yes, sacred sound realizes transitions into life and into death, envoicing the cosmologies, memories, and spaces of which it is part. Yes, sacred sound is historical and, at the same time, troubles historicism by bringing other-than-human agents from the past (and prophetic knowledge of the future) into the present.[18]

These affirmative yeses are meant to recognize how music and religion are disentangled and entangled in a certain story of ethnomusicological thinking.[19] Some of the first musicologies were sonic theologies[20] described in scriptural, poetic, and literary language:

- In the *Upanishads* (1st millennium BCE), the mantra OM (*Śabda-Brahman)* is set forth as the sound of the Supreme Absolute and generative of the universe.
- In the *Gītassarasutta* (likely 1st century BCE), a discourse from the *Aṅguttara Nikāya, bhikkhus* (monks) are admonished of the dangers of attachment to elaborate melodic recitation.
- In the *Tehillim* (the Psalms of David, 9th–5th centuries BCE), texts for singing in worship describe the melodies, instruments, vocal attitudes, and times of day, life, and the Jewish liturgical year for praise, lament, and thanksgiving.
- In the Pauline epistles (1st century CE), early Christian communities are urged to glorify God and forge spiritual unity in congregational song.
- In Sura 96 "Al-'Alaq" ("The Clot," 7th century CE), the Prophet Muhammad encounters the angel Jibril, who begins to reveal the Qur'ān to him, thereby centering aurality in Islamic practice.

Texts like these, in turn, shaped the thinking of figures like Purandara Dasa (16th century CE, a founder of the Carnatic music tradition in the Indian subcontinent), Yunqi Zhuhong (16th century CE, an apologist for *nianfo* Pure Land Buddhist recitation), Maimonides (12th century CE, an advocate for the permissibility of music in all quarters of Jewish life), Augustine (4th–5th century CE, a measured apologist for musical affect in Christian worship), al-Ghazālī (11th century CE, an Islamic philosopher of permissible musical affect), and Guru Nanak (15th–16th century CE, founder of Sikhism and composer of hymns in the *Guru Granth Sahib*) who are central to sacred musicological traditions in their own right. While contemporary music and sound scholars draw deeply on these touchstone figures and texts, they encounter them primarily as exegetic, contextualizing, authorizing voices positioned outside the histories and genealogies of much ethnomusicology. These are the phrases on the tips of ethnographic partners' tongues, the books on their shelves and apps on their mobile devices, the words of their prayers and liturgies, and the theories of sacred sound that authorize their traditions. They are subjects and objects of ethnomusicology, not ethnomusicology proper; profound theology, not critical social scientific and humanistic knowledge.[21] In broadest perspective, *Music and Religion* names and responds to historical and political conditions that differentiate and connect sacred musicologies and contemporary ethnomusicology.

To do this in the chapters that follow, I trace, perhaps predictably, the disciplinary turns in twentieth- and twenty-first-century ethnomusicologies that tell a story of the culturalist disentangling (Chapter 1) and nonsecular entangling (Chapter 2) of music and religion. These turns move not in a straight chronology, but as meandering, overlapping regions in a disciplinary Venn diagram. We move, in other words, from the comfortable absenting of other-than-human agents (including those produced by humans) and theological language to the transformative presencing of the same.[22] And put less abstractly, we move from the exclusion of ethnomusicologists (often religious practitioners and/or from the non-white global majority) who have knowledge of other-than-human agents and write in theological language to their gradual, belated recognition in the field. The historical and political conditions that frame these disciplinary turns, I suggest, can be understood through the complex, globally felt effects of and responses to religion as a modern, secular category of thought and social ordering.

Religion here is a kind of difference producing recognizable, legible, audible, tolerated spaces of practice and experience, thereby becoming a form of universalized, secular sameness. Religious difference as secular sameness, for the anthropologist Dipesh Chakrabarty, means that "if we could all have the same context, then we would all have the same gods" (2000: 76). The philosopher Santiago Castro-Gómez would call this kind of secular knowledge "the hubris of point zero" (2021; cited in Irving 2024: 10). In fact, gods and other-than-human agents have been written out of a secular ethnomusicology that encounters religion exclusively as culturalized difference. "Allowing only human protagonists into our stories," the anthropologist Anna Lowenhaupt Tsing writes, "is a cultural agenda tied to dreams of progress through modernization" (2015: 155).[23] By necessity, then, this project situates ethnomusicology within the capacious body of recent critical work on the modern concepts of religion and secularity.[24] Here, I listen for the enchantments of contemporary ethnomusicology—indeed, an "anointed" ethnomusicology (A. Jones 2020) in some of its nonsecular forms—emerging from the critique of religion I and many others write within.[25]

Since its beginnings in positivist ethnological and national/regional folklore collection projects[26] and fraught comparative musicological projects in the nineteenth and twentieth centuries,[27] ethnomusicology has had a deep, abiding connection to religion as a discrete category of practice and experience. In ethnomusicology, religion is ubiquitous—a self-evident claim borne out in the pages that follow.[28] The sacredness of sound (its material, ontological, and perceptual links to divine powers and right intentions) is a commonplace established, in part, through the globalized reach of Abrahamic and Dharmic traditions (Bohlman 2018). This commonplace has made it second-nature for ethnomusicologists to think in terms of religion—sometimes without enough distance from the transcendental aesthetics of European Romanticism that shape their habits of thought, sometimes while marginalizing practices that become "traditional religions."

But what about religion in the varied strands of ethnomusicological thinking? What might we gain in critically rethinking the making of religious genres, histories, repertoires, instruments, performers, and listeners or the common interpretive move of describing religious/secular/spiritual boundary maintenance and crossing? Unlike the concept of music, which has long been critiqued and rethought in light of different lexicons and ontologies and, more recently, as a discrete sonic object and kind of species-specific social practice within a broader field of sound, the concept of religion is, by and large, still taken as second-nature within much ethnomusicology. This is despite a rich body of social scientific and humanistic work examining religion's particular Enlightenment, colonial, and secular genealogies.

But, as I show in this project, there is an emerging sense of the extractive, colonizing tendencies of designations like Jewish music, music and Islam, Christian musical repertoires, or Vedic music theory, for instance. And, crucially, there are models of how ethnomusicologists have written with and against the concept of religion as they attune themselves to sacred voices and places, endeavor to be "with the gods in a musical way" (Friedson 2009: 8), and preserve in-between spaces in which they are neither "unwelcome inquisitors" in others' worlds nor renderers of those worlds in spaces ethnomusicologists "dominate utterly" (Jankowsky 2007: 191). *Music and Religion* is, then, a story of disciplinary renewal through a layering of the secular and nonsecular in ethnomusicological praxis.

Disentangling, Entangling

The disciplinary turns I trace here involve ethnomusicologists embracing, questioning, and transforming religion as a readymade, secular, second-nature epistemological and methodological frame. Put simply, I tell a story of ethnomusicology shifting (however incompletely and in fits and starts) from a post-Enlightenment secular approach disentangling religion and music along cultural lines to a nonsecular approach embracing the entanglements of humans and other-than-humans in ethnomusicological knowledge. Disentangling music and religion is a culturalist project that ethnomusicology has been invested in for most of its history. Entangling sound, deities and other-than-humans, sacred objects, and musicking, listening, researching subjects is an ethnomusicology that powerfully transforms the secular relationship of music and religion. *Music and Religion* traces a disciplinary renewal as the disentangling of those categories becomes less second-nature in ethnomusicology. As I suggest here, an entangled ethnomusicology continues to thrive in fulsome, decolonizing, antiracist disciplinary spaces that refuse religion's secular enclosure. And in certain resurgent ethnomusicologies, disentangling music and religion has not been a normative project. A crucial part of this story, then, is centering ethnomusicologists and ethnomusicologies that explicitly embrace, theorize, and practice the entanglements of music and religion or, better, *musicandreligion*. If a book titled *Music and Religion* perforce signifies disentangling, my hope is to also write beyond that historical and political moment to name a space of encounter and transformation where secular and nonsecular praxes braid together.

In a disentangled ethnomusicology, religion as a category of reflexive critique and theorizing is largely (and tellingly) absent in canonical reviews of the discipline, as a quick glance at most indexes demonstrates. In classic anthropological treatments of ethnomusicology in a rational/scientific vein, culturalist approaches define music as (nearly) exclusively human, with gods, spirits, demons, and other-than-humans disentangled from musical sound, behavior, and experience, often through the secular frame of religion.[29] In Alan Merriam's *The Anthropology of Music* (1964), music is species specific and culturally shaped; it "cannot be produced except by people for other people" (1964: 6). When music and religion intersect in Merriam's work, it is through the functionalist validation of religious systems and precepts in service of cultural and social stability (1964: 224–225). Drawing on his fieldwork experiences with Basongye communities to theorize how they conceived of musical and non-musical sound, Merriam holds fast to the singular role of human agency in a Basongye musical ontology:

> There is some difference among the Basongye as to whether the *bikudi*, or ancestral spirits, sing, but this is more a question of whether the singing can be heard rather than of whether music is produced. The elders say that on exceptional occasions the ancestral spirits can be heard singing in the bush at night, and this is consistent with the theory of music since ancestral spirits are conceived to be human and thus capable of making music. Younger men, however, say that the elders are foolish and that the night noises ascribed to the ancestral spirits are really the crying of the jackal and thus not singing at all; this again is consistent since animals cannot produce music of any kind. Finally, song is not part of myth or legend; although the ability to sing or play a music instrument comes directly from Efile Mukulu (God), Efile Mukulu is not conceived as a music producer in the sense that he sings himself, nor do the culture heroes involved in the creation of the earth and man sing in the course of their creative activities. Thus the idea that music is created only by humans is consistent within the framework of Basongye conception. (1964: 64–65)

Although Merriam immediately goes on to acknowledge the non-universality of music as an exclusively human field in the ethnographic record, he is eager to connect music to the performance and perception of humans in a Basongye musical ontology. This accords well with the methodological atheism (Berger 1967) of postwar social sciences that treated ascriptions of agency to other-than-humans as, ultimately, human activity (Geertz 1966). John Blacking's *How Musical Is Man?* (1973) continues in this vein, with his famous definitions of music as "humanly organized sound" and society as "soundly organized humanity" centering the human as the ultimate arbiter of what music is and does. In Venda possession dance (*ngoma dza midzumi*), then, "kinship is as important a factor as the rhythm of music in having effects on people" (1973: 45), but other-than-human agency does not weigh in Blacking's interest in efficacy.

Unlike most disciplinary theorizations, Marcia Herndon and Norma McLeod's *Music as Culture* (1980) explicitly names religion as a category in "the relationship of music to social institutions" (1980: 111–124). Herndon and McLeod emphasize the functions of musical structures and styles in the human action of religion: the effects of repetition, patterning, and redundancy within ritual performance and stable religious traditions; the efficacy of correct performance to reach "the ears of the supernatural" (1980: 114); and the creation of conditions for the "ecstatic and culture-bound" experience of trance (1980: 120). On the one hand, Herndon and McLeod's functionalist focus on music's sounding features leads them to treat other-than-human agency in the subjunctive: ". . . often said to have been handed down directly to men by the Gods" (1980: 114). On the other hand, they open space, at times, beyond functionalism to tentatively embrace other-than-human agency in relational forms of voice and listening: ". . . a non-human way of talking which can be understood in the spirit world" (1980: 114). In *Music as Culture*, Herndon and McLeod offer us glimpses of what entangling music and religion in ethnomusicological interpretation might mean.

True to their ethnomusicological moments, Merriam, Blacking, and Herndon and McLeod were primarily interested in non-Western alterity: music other than the Western/Christian/capitalist ontologies against which European and North American ethnomusicology tended to define itself. Theirs was an ethnomusicology caught up, to differing degrees (and by far not the most problematic examples), in the colonizing, extractive disciplinary practices that ethnomusicology continues to struggle with. Theirs was also an ethnomusicology committed to disentangling music and religion through methodological atheism or methodological agnosticism (Smart 1973);

ethnomusicology as a social science in which humans are musicians and sources of musical knowledge and other-than-human agency is not real or not knowable. Finally, theirs was an ethnomusicology yet to confront the crises of positionality, reflexivity, and representation that continue to unsettle and transform the discipline. For Merriam, Blacking, and Herndon and McLeod, disentangling music and religion was not only a project that centered the human, but also one that sidelined or swore off ethnomusicologists' relationships and experiences with humans and other-than-humans in the field to carry out a secularized "sciencing about music," in Merriam's words (1964: 25 cited in Titon 2008: 29).

In Bruno Nettl's iterative theorizing and historicizing of the field in *Theory and Method in Ethnomusicology* (1964) and the three editions of *The Study of Ethnomusicology* (1983, 2005, and 2015), we witness ethnomusicology's increasing comfort with the entanglement of music and religion, albeit firmly on the side of ethnographic interpretation rather than ethnomusicologists' positioned experiences. In other words, Nettl fully embraces other-than-human agency in music and religion, encountering and beholding invocations of divinity and the absolute through a methodological ludism (Bielo 2015: 38; Droogers 1999) that resists collapsing religious experiences and ontologies into secularized functionalism. Among music's uses and functions, Nettl places special emphasis on its role in mediating between "human and other beings" to sustain "humanity's relationship to the supernatural" (2015: 267). For Nettl, other-than-human beings are agents in sacred music histories and musicologies as well, teaching and revealing music to humans and intervening in their creative efforts (2015: 385). Nettl's embrace of entanglement is often on view: with respect to the Carnatic poet/composer/singer/saint Tyagaraja, Nettl emphasizes that, for many Indian musicologists, Tyagaraja's profound accomplishments must be "ascribed to divine beneficence" and "divine intervention" (2015: 58). And without qualification, Nettl encounters in Tyagaraja "the Indian musician's habit of long daily practice" commingling with "timely intercession of the deities, especially Rama" (2015: 59). Regarding the entanglement of music and religion in ethnomusicologists' lifeworlds and ways of knowing—a kind of methodological theism (Bielo 2015: 39–41)

I expand upon later in this book—Nettl is silent, however. For Nettl, an ethnomusicologist's positioning with regard to religious ways of knowing and nonsecular methodologies was not a pressing concern for the field.

Indeed, in contrast with anthropology's theorizing of "belief-inclusive research" (Pohran 2022), the question of ethnomusicologists' positions in terms of religious ways of knowing and nonsecular methodologies is not explicitly addressed in most recent disciplinary theorizing: Harris M. Berger and Ruth M. Stone's *Theory for Ethnomusicology: Histories, Conversations, Insights* (2019) and Timothy Rice's *Modeling Ethnomusicology* (2017), for example. Gregory Barz and Timothy Cooley's editions of *Shadows in the Field: New Perspectives for Fieldwork in Ethnomusicology* (1997, 2008) are guided by the conviction that ethnomusicology must shift from representation to experience. To get there, ethnomusicologists model phenomenological, embodied, reflexive, performative ways of doing musical ethnography attuned to power and ethics in relationships that form in the field and sustain beyond. But fieldwork experience in *Shadows in the Field* is limited to the human (other-than-human beings cast no shadows, apparently). To put it another way, the methodological and theoretical concerns of the moments the two editions mark are grounded in a secular approach to religion; when religion matters, it matters as a culturalized category of difference similar to the other kinds of difference the authors engage. In this meditation on experiential ethnomusicology, other-than-human agents and relationships are not written in (including nonhumans, objects, and places beyond the frame of religion).

In 2011, religious studies scholar Rosalind Hackett noted that, in her field, "an auditory or acoustic turn is only now taking shape" (2011: 447) but, referencing *Shadows in the Field*, worried that the ethnomusicological expertise needed for "substantive participation" (Barz and Cooley 2008: 5) in religious worlds could have a "chilling effect" on the belatedly emerging turn to sound in religious studies (Hackett 2011: 454). This is one of the spaces and moments for ethnomusicology, and music studies and sonically oriented anthropology more generally, to intervene transformatively in the acoustic/auditory turn in religious studies and beyond.

At the risk of immodesty, I will mention here how my involvement in naming religion as a space for theorizing in ethnomusicology and music studies might contribute to integrating critiques of secularity in the humanities and social sciences and the expertise of those at home in working with music and sound. As some scholars have noted (Kärjä 2022: 26; Laack 2015: 226), it was only in the second edition of Martin Clayton, Trevor Herbert, and Richard Middleton's *The Cultural Study of Music: A Critical Introduction* (2012) that religion became a discrete field for theorizing and critique (Engelhardt 2012). In that short piece, out of which this book emerges, I linger over the epistemological challenges and methodological imperatives of encountering religion beyond a secular, culturalized frame. I point to the question of sound's sacrality per se and the difference-rendering potentials of religious faith and experience as openings, not impossibilities, for relational knowing through sound. Ontological difference is essential here: an openness to the possibility that ontology is not just or not only cultural (Viveiros de Castro 1998), even as we write in the language of secular critique.

This brings us, I suggest, to a moment of articulation in the disciplinary story I tell: the provocation of no scare quotes. What methodologically atheist or methodologically agnostic ethnomusicologists once placed in scare quotes ("voice of a deity" or "divine audition") might, in an entangled, nonsecular ethnomusicology, be the voice of a deity or divine audition, without scare quotes or disciplinary suspicion. This book goes beyond my contribution in *The Cultural Study of Music* in two key ways. First, I embrace a flat ontology in which humans and other-than-humans are equally agents (capable of producing effects without something anterior) in the worlds ethnomusicologists inhabit. Second, I extend what an entangled, nonsecular ethnomusicology might mean into the worlds of ethnomusicologists whose methodologies are explicitly and reflexively theistic.

(Un)bracketing Religion, Ethnomusicologically

In working our way through key histories and theorizations of culturalist ethnomusicology, we arrive, through the proverbial disciplinary turns, at a current moment when ethnomusicology is being reshaped by critiques of religion as a secular frame and an openness to what nonsecular methodologies and modes of representation might be. The Society for Ethnomusicology's Religion, Music, and Sound section (founded first as a special interest group in 2010), the *Yale Journal of Music & Religion* (founded in 2014), the Congregational Music Studies series (founded with Ashgate in 2013 and with Routledge since 2016), the Music and Performance in Muslim Contexts series with Edinburgh University Press (founded in 2022), *Musica Judaica* (founded in 1974), Istanbul University Press's *Meshk Journal of Religious Music* (founded in 2024), and the Society for Christian Scholarship in Music (founded in 2003) are examples of these kinds of religion-centered initiatives within or significantly intersecting with ethnomusicology. The journal *Black Sacred Music*, published from 1987–1995 and edited by Yahya Jongintaba (formerly known as Jon Michael Spencer), also deserves special mention here as it sought to imagine and practice a theologically informed musicology, or theomusicology.

The story I tell here begins with discussions of music and singing in Bernard Picart and Jean Frédéric Bernard's *Cérémonies et coutumes religieuses de tous le peuples du monde* (*The Religious Ceremonies and Customs of the Several Nations of the Known World*, 1723–1737), a watershed, sympathetic Enlightenment compendium of religious practices in the secular vein of world religions (see Chapter 1). My story moves through the atheistic, agnostic, and ludic methodologies of twentieth- and twenty-first-century ethnomusicologies and encounters the expanding spaces of nonsecular ethnomusicology epitomized by recent work in the Black gospel tradition (see Chapter 2).[30] To put a finer point on it, my story is one in which entangled, nonsecular ethnomusicologies incorporating the knowledge of other-than-human relationships and theistic methodologies constitute antiracist, decolonizing, epistemologically and methodologically nuanced interventions in what ethnomusicology might become and who is recognized as an ethnomusicologist.

To locate the transitions between the disentangled and entangled ethnomusicologies I am thinking about, I will spend a moment here contrasting work that represents those approaches and sets the stage for the two central chapters of this book. Jeff Todd Titon and Melvin Butler are ethnomusicologists who theorize positionality, stance, belief, and secular/nonsecular praxes with great care in their scholarship. Titon's twentieth-century and Butler's twenty-first-century work offer us compelling models of disentangled and entangled ethnomusicologies inhabiting the divergent soundscapes of Baptist and Pentecostal Christianities in the United States and the Caribbean. Titon, whose work I would characterize as secure in its agnostic methodology, is committed to bracketing off religious experience and other-than-human agency in understanding "people making music" (1996: xxii).[31] Butler, whose work I would characterize as verging with a light touch into methodological theism, is committed to integrating his life as "an academic and spiritual being" (2000: 38) through an epistemology grounded in musicking and the Holy Spirit. For a fuller accounting of how Titon's and Butler's held identities and positions shape their work, one must, of course, engage with the richness of their scholarship as a whole.

In *Powerhouse for God: Speech, Chant, and Song in an Appalachian Baptist Church* (2018 [1988]) and multiple theoretical reflections on ethnomusicological fieldwork in religious communities,[32] Titon makes the case for a disentangled ethnomusicology that is deeply sympathetic to accounts of other-than-human agency in musical creation and other-than-human relationship in religious experience. At the same time, Titon, informed by decades of fieldwork with Baptist and Pentecostal Christians in the United States, approaches "religious belief and practice as a cultural system" (1991: 5)—religion as a secular form of difference in the culturalist vein familiar to ethnomusicology. Religion is not a different kind of difference, in other words. Titon's conviction is that a Husserlian bracketing of other-than-human agency and experiences of the sacred within the frame of culture is essential to ethnomusicology as a social science (as opposed to theology): "I mean to be phenomenologically agnostic, 'bracketing' or setting aside the question of whether their worldview is true or false outside of their cultural setting while representing them as if it is true within it" (1991: 9 and also see Titon 2018: 477–478 and 2021a: 65). This means that Titon encounters the testimony of someone like Brother Belvin Hurt receiving a gospel song from the Holy Spirit (Titon 1980) as an element of religious belief to be examined for its relationship with musical behavior (Titon 1985: 20): the divine as warrant for human action. Ethnographic accounts of other-than-human agency are bracketed and disentangled, with Titon moving on to an ethnomusicological analysis of the structure and lyrical content of Brother Hurt's song apart from his "passive role" (Titon 1980: 228) in the composition process under the "anointment of the Spirit" (1980: 226). Might the "unusual" (1980: 226) structure of Brother Hurt's gospel song be attributable to the Holy Spirit, one wonders?

No, not in an ethnomusicology where other-than-human agency is bracketed off, the humanness of musicking is definitive, and testimonies like Brother Hurt's become part of worldviews and culture. The bracketing moves of an agnostic methodology reserve the social scientific takeaways for human-centered explanations. "No ethnomusicologist could maintain a scholarly reputation," Titon suggests, "if he attributed the cause of the religious music and behavior he observed in the field to God. Instead, scholarly reputations have been built on insisting the opposite" (1985: 22).

But Titon is also unsatisfied with the exclusive secularity of a scientific paradigm that "must absolutely reject all absolutist claims to truth" (1985: 23). In later work, Titon seeks to understand the breath-based integration of Old Regular Baptist congregational singing in eastern Kentucky being "tuned up with the grace of God"; "in step and deliberately just a bit out of phase" (2006: 320). Early on, Titon did not apprehend how Old Regular Baptists' language of religious experience "might serve as an explanation of what I considered a technical problem: the integration in their music" (2006: 326). After some time, however, Titon arrives at a different place: "Was it really metaphor when they spoke of being tuned up with the grace of God? When they spoke of how the Holy Spirit made a melody? Or was it not metaphor at all but their habitual ways of thinking, their quite literal belief?" (2006: 328).

This might be as far as an agnostic, disentangled ethnomusicology can take us without admitting the agency of other-than-humans and replacing belief with knowledge. By listening for and identifying Old Regular Baptists' "unerring sense for a long period" (2006: 330), Titon brings us to the musicalization of their belief in a divine presence through their singing. Their belief is still bracketed in relativist, cultural terms, however. Religion is, in Titon's final analysis, disentangled in the disciplinary norms of a secular ethnomusicology, mapping onto a classic emic/etic distinction (Herndon 1993) at the boundary of religious belief. Religion-as-belief, then, is a frame that fundamentally shapes Titon's ethnomusicology, which means excluding the agency of other-than-humans in an ethnomusicological paradigm.[33] While Titon is quick to point out that the difference across which the bracketing of belief operates is productive,[34] he leaves us at a firmly drawn disciplinary boundary: "By resolutely projecting my role and maintaining my identity as a professional ethnomusicologist," Titon writes, "I take my place among the unsaved" (1985: 18).

But what about the professional ethnomusicologist who has a place among the saved (Butler 2019: 2) in a community of religious belonging and practice; whose "epistemological home" (2019: 13) is at once inside the discipline of ethnomusicology and the world of Pentecostal saints, in Melvin Butler's case? In *Island Gospel: Pentecostal Music and Identity in Jamaica and the United States* (2019) and multiple theoretical meditations on "observant participation" (cf. Tedlock 1991) as a believing scholar,[35] Butler models what a theistic methodology can mean for ethnomusicology. "Because I share the religious beliefs of those whom I am studying," Butler writes, "I must necessarily hold, for example, that the Holy Spirit is indeed real and is manifested through music. Furthermore, this manifestation is not subject to an individual's 'belief' in it, nor is it limited to the 'worldview' of a particular group of people" (2000: 38). For Butler, there is no bracketing of other-than-human agency, his religious experience, and the religious experiences of those he works with in an entangled ethnomusicology. His is a flat ontology in which other-than-humans are agents and in relationship with humans not as artifacts of belief but as part of the real; Butler views a culturalist approach in which religious beliefs and worldviews are attributes of secular difference as "ontological colonialism" (2000: 38). What is bracketed in an entangled, nonsecular ethnomusicology, in other words, is the question of cultural difference.

This effects a shift in perspective regarding questions that vex a secular ethnomusicology: questions of epistemology and ethnographic limits that are erased or bracketed through atheistic, agnostic, and ludic methodologies. Butler describes a moment of "observation-as-worshiping" at the Glorious Rock Worship Center in Port-au-Prince, Haiti when

> a woman at the front right side of the sanctuary began to flail her arms and let out a series of shrieks. Falling to the ground and out of the view of all but those next to her, the woman was experiencing either the joyous touch of the Holy Spirit or an attack of an evil spirit—at least those are the two options into which most churchgoers would relegate her experience. But other Haitian Christians see the woman's apparently involuntary behavior in more nuanced terms. Perhaps it evidenced a spiritual experience more properly situated in the cracks of a rigid holy-evil dichotomy. Or perhaps this was, heaven forbid, a learned behavior—a *performance* of Pentecostal faith motivated by a desire to express a natural emotion. (2016: 615–616)

A secular approach to this moment moves quickly to questions of the veracity and pragmatism of the woman's experience of or response to "heated" worship. In this paradigm, her actions were either (1) an authentic expression of "spiritual transcendence" (a term Butler prefers to "trance" or "possession" given his "belief in the validity of Pentecostal experiences in general" [2002: 93 n9; also see 2008b: 56 n2]) and, therefore, bracketed beyond what is knowable, or (2) a functional "distractive outburst" (2016: 617) through which she could navigate the social and spiritual textures of the moment. For Butler the "Pentecostal researcher" and "researching Pentecostal" (2019: 13), however, this moment landed differently. Given the reality of other-than-human agents, Butler does not need to jump to questions of veracity and pragmatism: the presence of the Holy Spirit in that moment is not contingent on human belief or the authentic manifestation of spiritual transcendence. Instead, Butler's entangled ethnomusicology leads him to a critically nuanced understanding of the woman's "distractive outburst as an element contributing to the worship service's success. It may have served to outline the limits of exuberance and/or as constructive evidence of the tangibility of spiritual forces" (2016: 617). What gets him there? "My past experiences in a wide variety of heated worship services," Butler writes,

> had prepared me *not* to know, to accept the uncertainty of it; I had gained a level of intellectual comfort that, despite (or perhaps because of) my allegiance to the faith, the "legitimacy" of these kinds of practices—the question of whether they really "are" spiritual manifestations—must lie outside my analytical frame. (2016: 616)

I read this "outside" not as an agnostic bracketing off of religion but as an outcome of Butler's epistemology of faith. Could one understand the effects of the woman's actions with such critical nuance within a secular ethnomusicology? Certainly so, and that is precisely my point here: on par with the pedigree of disentangled ethnomusicology's interpretive claims, an entangled ethnomusicology can arrive at a critical understanding of religious musicking whose place within the discipline is untroubled and untroubling. Without trying to represent another's subjective experience and lifeworld (or dispel the reality of other-than-human agency by reducing the woman's actions to performance), Butler unites epistemological humility and the reality of other-than-human agency known through not-unscientific methods of experience (2021: 184). His alternation between first- and third-person ethnography is one of the ways Butler negotiates a theistic methodology, weaving together the "I" of experiential and faith-born knowledge with the "they" of theological and positional difference (2002: 94–95, n12).[36] For Butler, music is the sounding of human/other-than-human relationships irreducible to culture, and his non-secular approach is part of a broader turn in ethnomusicology that opens the discipline to networks of actors, ways of musical knowing, and positioned research less exclusive of other-than-human beings.[37]

Coming to Terms and the Shape of Things to Come

Titon's and Butler's work illustrates the differences across which disentangled and entangled ethnomusicologies operate. As we move from the first chapter of *Music and Religion* ("Disentangling Religion") to the second ("Entangling Religion"), it is clear that these differences do not map onto a disciplinary chronology, since disentangled and entangled ethnomusicologies overlap one another into the present.[38] After all, hints of entanglement can be discerned in early ethnomusicology (e.g., David McAllester's 1954 *Enemy Way Music: A Study of Social and Esthetic Values as Seen in Navaho Music*), and important work progresses apace in a more disentangled mode (e.g., Anna Schultz's 2013 *Singing a Hindu Nation: Marathi Devotional Performance and Nationalism*). Nor do the differences relate primarily to repertoire, history, geography, or religious tradition (however uncomfortably we hold that term). Rather, the differences between disentangled and entangled ethnomusicologies reside, I suggest, in the positionalities and recognition of ethnomusicologists themselves. Religious knowing is embodied, which means it is racialized, gendered, and resides in voice, sexuality, abilities and disabilities, class, and the other ways humans are in the world differently. Simply put, as nonsecular methodologies and epistemologies (re)enter ethnomusicology, their practitioners and bearers transform the discipline because of who they are. In the global histories of discoursing, writing, theologizing, and knowing about sound's entanglement with religion, what we encounter as a resurgence of nonsecular ethnomusicology is a major part of the discipline's belated, ongoing coming to terms with decolonial, antiracist, "more-than-Eurological" (Bissett Perea 2021: 9) urgencies. If the resurgence of a nonsecular, entangled ethnomusicology unsettles past understandings of the field and opens onto a methodologically and epistemologically more fulsome future (a future that also includes work in secular, disentangled traditions, of course), then that is a good thing. Fields like anthropology, history, and religious studies have come around the "post-secular" turn and thrived, and surely ethnomusicology (and music studies as a whole) can do the same. I write more about what that future entails in the conclusion of *Music and Religion*.

Here, I have to say some words about how I define ethnomusicology and whom I include in these pages. The nature of the disciplinary story I tell in *Music and Religion* means that my focus is on the ethnomusicological tradition I inhabit: English-dominant, Eurological with genealogies inextricably bound to colonization, missionization, imperialism, and secular reason, and with a center of institutional gravity in North America. As I mention above, this ethnomusicological tradition emerges from and is in ongoing dialogue with sacred musicologies and other ethnomusicological traditions, many of which now inform a nonsecular resurgence. My own work, shaped by a childhood in the Methodist congregation my father pastored and my mother's work in a divinity school, has, mostly unwittingly, represented a bit of ethnomusicology's accumulating entanglement. In *Singing the Right Way: Orthodox Christians and Secular Enchantment in Estonia* (2015), for instance, I did something I write about in Chapter 2: taking a theological concept and using it for purposes of ethnomusicological theorizing, perhaps to be taken up by others in situations far removed from mine, just like the purported universality of secular critical theory. For the Orthodox Estonians I wrote about, singing the right way was at the heart of their sacramental relationship with God. Orthodoxy, *õigeusk* or *ortodoks* in Estonian, can be parsed as both "right belief" and "right glory/worship." To believe correctly is to worship correctly; to follow the apostolic tradition of the church is to ethically form one's religious subjectivity the right way. In this feedback loop of orthodoxy and orthopraxy, what a nonsecular ethnomusicology does *not* require is establishing the "real" derivation of an ethics of style (Rommen 2007) apart from theology and Orthodoxy's central mysteries. Critical assessments of style, voice, history, ideology, and institutional power matter, of course, but they do not explain away the ethnographic fact of divine agency in theological knowledge.[39]

I am not Orthodox, a fact that my Orthodox friends' and research partners' musical and theological "boundary work" (Gidal 2016) often reminds me of, and I cannot adopt, obviously, the theistic methodology of an Orthodox Christian. But, in my uptake and application of theology, I am theistic-curious, or perhaps at the theistic end of an agnostic methodological spectrum. This is a point I will return to in the conclusion of this book, and state here as well: an entangled ethnomusicology's theistic methodologies recognize both the reality of gods, spirits, deities, and demons (often through ethnomusicologists' relationships with them) and the reality of their agency (which does not require encountering their presence or "belief"). The historian Dipesh Chakrabarty makes this point otherwise:

> I take gods and spirits to be existentially coeval with the human, and I think from the assumption that the question of being human

> involves the question of being with gods and spirits. Being human means, as Ramachandra Gandhi puts it, discovering "the possibility of calling upon God [or gods] without being under an obligation to first establish his [or their] reality." (2000: 16)

At the Mt. Calvary Holy Church Christian Restoration Centre in Nairobi, Martha and the assembled women prepared themselves to hear about chama participation by envoicing their relationships to God as praise-singing subjects and recognizing God's (potential) agency in their lives. Others, no doubt, sang themselves, tentatively, into emerging relationships of risk, trust, and obligation that were only obliquely, or not at all, about their relationships to God and shaped by God's agency. At the beginning of this Introduction, I suggest a both/and approach to encountering this moment ethnomusicologically. It is functionalist and worship. It recognizes the authority of God, Martha, her pastor husband, and the NGO staff and the women's inchoate relationships by their response to Martha's calls. And it makes the women's time, vocal energies, moving bodies, religious selves, and financial situations musically oriented toward the chama information session and sign-up that followed.

What it was not—and this brings me to some of the commonplace binaries in the study of music and religion I write against here—was *either* sacred *or* secular, spiritual *or* material, entangled *or* disentangled, Christian *or* Muslim, a space of God's agentive presence *or* suspect absence, religious *or* non-religious. Contradictions abound in these either/or, 0/1 binaries, after all. The Eurological concept of religion is secular (to write in terms of religion is a secular undertaking), and its aptness in spaces like the Mt. Calvary Holy Church Christian Restoration Centre is open to question. Mapambio call-and-response singing is neither religious nor non-religious but an everyday vocal practice expressing human joys and sorrows and relationships to human and other-than-human beings (Barz 2005: 5–6). Agency, a potential to produce effects in the world without something anterior, was distributed throughout the Mt. Calvary Holy Church Christian Restoration Centre, including both the gathered women and a God whose agency is not contingent on presence or absence (Gell 1998). Other-than-human agency, in other words, is not contingent on the real presence of an other-than-human being.[40] Finally, a disentangled ethnomusicology that holds music and religion at arm's length from each other can cultivate a feel for the inadequacies of those reifications, inviting one to encounter the entanglements of *musicandreligion.*

This project traces shifts in ethnomusicology that reach to the discipline's epistemological core. If a secular ethnomusicology brackets off other-than-human agency in musicking and musical knowing to render religion as one more form of culturalist difference (Chapter 1), then a nonsecular ethnomusicology reorients the field around equally agentive humans and other-than-humans (Chapter 2). While new materialism's flat ontologies, vibrant matter, and networks of actors are not contained by the category of religion, ethnomusicologists' desires to listen to and know religion's other-than-human agents have precipitated the disciplinary transformations I write about here.[41] Many have voiced a sense of crisis across ethnographic disciplines that to do ethnography is to do secularity with its pitfalls of colonial extraction and sovereign-seeming reason,[42] and ethnomusicologists may be, implicitly, voicing similar concerns. The promise of ethnomusicology's nonsecular turn, I offer, is this: not only can ethnomusicologists know about the musically human in a Blackingesque mode, but they can also know about humans' sonic and ontological entanglements with other-than-human beings and, perhaps, know something about other-than-human beings themselves through the sounds they hear, receive, and respond to.[43] In the call-and-response singing at the Mt. Calvary Holy Church Christian Restoration Centre, we can know musically about those women, about the effects of their praise, and about their God in a theologically inflected, humanist ethnomusicology. If not a point of arrival for the discipline as a whole, this theological horizon is a beacon for reading ethnomusicology's histories and writing its futures.

To close, I pivot into the next chapters with some provocations relating to time-honored ethnomusicological issues:

- Are gods, spirits, divinities, and demons present (and captive) in archives, museums, notation, and other media forms? What are our obligations to them?

- In an entangled ethnomusicology, what are the limits of sound- and image-capturing technologies and the circulation of their media?
- How do ethnomusicologists account for other-than-human agency (agency that may precede its sonic expression) in musical affect and emotion?
- What is a musical/sonic equivalent of the distinction between literature and scripture? Writing and calligraphy?
- Is there a musical/sonic equivalent of a sacred relic?
- In a disentangled ethnomusicology, when might critical ethnography become religious blasphemy?[44] How might doing ethnomusicology become an undesirable form of attachment or distraction?
- How might other-than-human agency intersect with Mantle Hood's bi-musicality model (1960)?
- Does other-than-human agency alter how payment and offering work in sonic/spiritual economies?
- What is a nonsecular ethnomusicological listening?
- How do ethnomusicologists encounter the non-sonic powers of religious music?
- Is taking ontologies and other-than-human beings seriously sufficient within current ethnomusicological paradigms?
- Does an entangled ethnomusicology attempt to skirt questions of sovereign refusal and the presumption of access across colonial and racial asymmetries?

I hope this book might reframe and reanimate these questions in generative ways . . .

Notes

1. I am thankful to Olive Murage for her help in translating from Kiswahili.
2. On the ethically neutral dynamics of collective/collected singing, particularly in the play of prolepsis (representing a future figured in the present) and parabasis (interruption and digression) in call-and-response practices, see Engelhardt et al. 2022.
3. See Eisenlohr (2024) on the atmospheric "half-things" (fleeting phenomena that come and go) that sonically intermingle between religious spaces and a "felt-body" that exceeds its physical boundaries.

4. The anthropologist Charles Hirschkind draws special attention to religion's "moral skepticism in regard to sonority": "Emerging during the seventeenth and eighteenth centuries, as one in the constellation of categories that together gave shape to what we now recognize as a modern moral and political order, religion is understood first and foremost to be a matter of belief, of the silent affirmation of religious truths within the private, inner space of individual subjectivity." And later: "Within the context of European colonialism, this same criterion undergirds the distinction between the religious lives of Europeans (quiet) and the forms of so-called primitive religion (noisy) said to be characteristic of non-Europeans" (2015: 165).
5. The enclosure of religion as set apart from modern secular society is another artifact of what Ana María Ochoa Gautier, following Latour and Bauman and Briggs, calls "epistemologies of purification" (2006) that seek to separate autonomous domains from social domains. This is part of a broader secular/colonial project that, as An Yountae reminds us, produced one secular category (race) out of another (religion): "The invention of race—as a constitutive element of coloniality—cannot be articulated apart from the history of the emergence of the concept of religion as the traditional lines demarcating ontological difference between people shifted from religious language (religious difference) to the secular language of scientific reason (racial difference)" (2024: 7).
6. There is a large literature on religion's insufficiency as a secular concept, but see Chidester 2014; Lambek 2008: 120–125; and Smith 1998 as points of departure.
7. From the extensive literature on ritual, Bell 1992 and Rappaport 1999 are especially apt for my writing here. Also see Coleman 2022 for a consideration of ritual indifference, fragmentation, and role ambiguity.
8. For work that illustrates the possible incommensurability of religion and sacred practices, see, for instance, Bohlman 2008, Brabec de Mori 2015, J. Jones 2013, Narayan 2016, Roseman 1991, and Srinivas 2018.
9. At the intersections of the material and sensorial turns in religious studies and ethnomusicology, see Blanton 2015, Diao 2023, Douglas 2020, Eisenlohr 2018, Hirschkind 2006, Meyer 2009, Promey 2014, and Stolow 2013. In the twentieth century, Fernando Ortiz's five-volume *Los instrumentos de la música afrocubana* (1952–1955) functions as an organology of "fetishistic objects" (Pavez Ojeda 2021: 127) linking specific materialities with the purity of cult value or denatured mercantilism. For select translations of Ortiz's writing on organology and religion, see Moore 2018.
10. Compare, for instance, Binson-Sumrongthong 2009, Engelhardt 2015, Harkness 2014, Nelson 1985, Sanga 2013, Summit 2016a, and Wong 2001.
11. Throughout *Music and Religion*, I write in terms of knowledge rather than belief, mindful of Marshall Sahlins's admonition that "the ethnographic 'believe' is often an ethnocentric reality check on what the people actually *know*" (2022: 13). For more on this knowledge, see Becker 2004, Feld 1982, Jankowsky 2010, Orsi 2005, and Seeger 1987.
12. On these communities, see J. Chen 2021, Harnish and Rasmussen 2011, Ingalls 2018, and Rasmussen 2010.
13. On these structures and flows, see Kapchan 2007, Mall 2021, and Qureshi 1986.
14. On this aspect of religion's social function, see Lorea 2023b and Sherinian 2014.
15. The literature historicizing and critiquing religion as a modern, Eurological category is vast, but my thinking here is indebted particularly to Asad 1993, Masuzawa 2005, Orsi 2016, Sahlins 2022, Taylor 2007, van der Veer 2014, and Weiss 2019: 8–19.
16. On the position of music in ethnomusicology and music studies, see Bohlman 1999; Meizel and Daughtry 2019; Nettl 2015: 19–30; Sakakeeny 2015; and Steingo and Sykes 2019.

17. In a similar vein, Guy Beck writes in *Musicology of Religion* against the binary of "window theory" (music and religion as windows on a transcendent, supernatural realm) and "mirror theory" (music and religion as mirrors of human projection and social construction) in twentieth- and twenty-first-century religious studies (2023: 18–21). Philip Bohlman and I do similar work in disrupting the transcendence/immanence binary in our introduction to *Resounding Transcendence: Transitions in Music, Religion, and Ritual* (2016).
18. In *Thinking with Ngangas*, Stephan Palmié comments that "admitting the spirits of dead people into our present so as to give testimony of and for the past that was their life violates the principle of anachronism. The minute they arrive, they would seem to contaminate the present with the past. In something of an inversion of the historian's cardinal sin of presentism, the unwitting backward projection of present concerns into the past, they throw the semiotics of historicism into disarray" (2023: 146). Michel-Rolph Trouillot makes the same point in *Silencing the Past:* subjects do not succeed a past but are its contemporaries (1995: 16).
19. In *Sacred and Secular Musics: A Postcolonial Approach,* Virinder S. Kalra rightly cautions against an easy resolution of the disentangled/entangled dynamic through recourse to a universal category of the sacred: "In considering the cauldron of colonial modernity out of which classification of music and religion emerges, the evocation of the sacred is too easy an escape out of the molten mixtures that burn into and imprint on the precolonial landscape" (2015: 8).
20. Contemporary scholars writing explicitly in the rehabilitated language of sonic theology (see Chapter 2) include Alter 2019; Beck 1993; Gerety 2016, 2020; Goshadze 2025; Hagedorn 2006, 2017; Neusner 1995; Shelley 2021; and Williams 2020.
21. As will become clear as *Music and Religion* develops, my rough characterization here is, in part, a lament that the Eurologics of secular, English-dominant ethnomusicology have excluded scholars and ways of knowing from other, global-majority, perhaps nonsecular traditions of music studies. What will also become clear as this book develops is my celebration of expanding spaces for nonsecular methodologies and ways of knowing within a more fulsome and, ultimately, more relationally and positionally sophisticated ethnomusicology. For a sense of the possibilities of "other musicologies" (Qureshi 1999) beyond the Eurological and the secular, see, for instance, Agawu 2023, 2003; Bakhle 2005; Bissett Perea 2021; Blum 2013; Diamond 2013; Kalra 2015; Ochoa Gautier 2014; Robinson 2020; and Williams 2019, 2022, 2024.
22. Even as, extending Luhrmann (2020), ethnomusicology's "invisible" others have not, in the discipline's history, been inaudible, except when their other-than-human sounds are, indeed, unheard by human beings. This accords with approaches to religion as mediation; as "attempts to render the invisible as *somehow visible* and the elusive as *somehow tangible* through forming and promoting embodied practices that shape what and how people see and sense" (Meyer and Stordalen 2019b: 5).
23. Throughout this book, I am indebted to ethnomusicological work examining other-than-human agency in music adjacent to and apart from religion per se. This includes new materialist scholarship on musical instruments (Bates 2012, 2019; Dirksen 2019; Douglas 2020; Piekut 2014; Roda 2014; Şenay 2020; Wolf 2014) and work explicitly addressing other-than-human agency (Brabec de Mori 2017; Kolar 2020).
24. Here, too, the literature is vast. My thinking is indebted to Asad 2003; Bielo 2015; Casanova 1994; Chakrabarty 2000; Goshadze 2025; Mahmood 2005; Masuzawa 2005; Orsi 2005, 2016; Taylor 2007; and van der Veer 2014.
25. Here I am thinking particularly of Bakhle 2008; Engelhardt 2015; Kalra 2015; Laack 2015; and Sykes 2018, 2020.

26. See Blum 1991: 3–10 and Nettl 2010: 22–32 for accounts of ethnomusicology's positivist histories.
27. See Nettl 2013, Ochoa Gautier 2014, and Stokes 2018 on ethnomusicology's fraught comparative projects.
28. Timothy Rice places the emergence of religion as a discrete focus of ethnomusicological attention in the 1960s (2017: 26).
29. Elsewhere in music studies, the exclusive humanness of music and music historiography was presented as axiomatic well into the twenty-first century: "No historical event or change can be meaningfully asserted unless its agents can be specified; and *agents can only be people.* Attributions of agency unmediated by human action are, in effect, lies—or at the very least, evasions" (Taruskin 2005: xviii).
30. Building on the reflexive, nonsecular praxis of William T. Dargan (1982) and Mellonee Burnim (1985), this growing body of work includes Barron 2020; Butler 2019; A. Jones 2020; Reed 2012; and Shelley 2021, 2023.
31. In the 2010s and 2020s, Titon's work has shifted toward "beings making sound" in the context of ecomusicology (Personal communication, 1/11/24).
32. See Titon 1980, 1985, 1991, 2006, and 2021a for his reflections on fieldwork, phenomenology, and religious difference.
33. In recent work on human and nonhuman sonic communication, Titon moves in a different direction, adopting a perspectivist approach while stopping short of enfolding other-than-human agency in an ethnomusicology of people making music. "Both human and nonhuman animals," Titon writes, "are subjects or persons to themselves and their conspecifics, even as they apprehend reality from different viewpoints" (2021b: 103).
34. See Titon 1985: 19 and 1991: 8 on the nuance this brings to essentialisms of religious insiders/outsiders.
35. See Butler 2000, 2002, 2008a, 2008b, 2014, 2016, 2021, and 2023 for the sweep of his methodologically theistic ethnomusicology.
36. See Butler 2008a: 99–100 on his religious and racial positionality in relation to traditional, place-based ethnography.
37. This turn includes Titon's recent work in eco-ethnomusicology (2015a, 2015b, 2019, 2020).
38. In an effort to rein in the scale of this project, I structure my story here primarily around the work of self-identifying ethnomusicologists, leaving many scholars in music studies, sound studies, anthropology, religious studies, and history whose work matters outside these pages. When I do engage with scholars beyond the field of ethnomusicology, I indicate their disciplinary affiliations.
39. This assertion is what motivated the subtitle of my book, parsed both ways as an interpretive device throughout its pages: *secular* enchantment (histories matter, although secular is a quality of time and knowledge, not the opposite of sacred) and secular *enchantment* (divine sonic presence matters, not least in its powers of salvation and relativizing the secular).
40. Marshall Sahlins might counter, however, that "being is being there" (2022: 39).
41. Echoing Robert Orsi, I place human relationships with other-than-human beings at the center my thinking about religion. "I can think of no religious world—not even Buddhism!," Orsi writes, "that does not offer practitioners opportunities to form deep ties with saints, ancestors, demons, gods, ghosts, and other special beings, in whose company humans work on the world and on themselves" (2005: 2).
42. For a sense of this conversation, see Lambek 2008, Lemons 2018, Mittermaier 2021, and Robbins 2020.
43. Knowing something about other-than-human beings can and must, of course, entail the epistemic decolonization of not knowing and not accessing. In this vein,

apophatic or negative theology, "Godly ethnography" (Moll 2023) that encounters the unknowability of the more-than-human, sitting with emptiness and impermanence (Chen 2001), the extravital and extraterrestrial extent of sound (Gerety 2021), and the (un)consciousness of nonbeing (Kuang 2019) are essential limits on positive, extractive forms of ethnomusicological knowing.

44. See Asad et al. 2009 for an extensive conversation on this subject.

1
Disentangling Religion

There are many possible moments for locating the proto-ethnomusicological origins of thinking about music and religion. The one I begin with here, Bernard Picart (1673–1733) and Jean-Frédéric Bernard's (1680–1744) seven-volume, 3000-plus page *Religious Ceremonies and Customs of All the Peoples of the World,* published in English with over 250 engraved plates in 1733–1739 (see Figure 1.1),[1] has been overlooked in work on Enlightenment attitudes toward religion in connection with the long emergence of ethnomusicology as a field. This is despite the fact that *Religious Ceremonies of the World* is a monument to the comparative desire (and colonizing force) that invents religion as a global phenomenon. The project secularized and relativized Eurocentric claims on the absolute (themselves intensely contested between Catholics, Protestants, and non-Christians) through what was, for the time, a sympathetic, tolerant approach. In their images and descriptions, Picart, the renowned engraver, and Bernard, the publisher and behind-the-scenes editor, compiler, and author of the project, modeled an Enlightenment disentangling of religion into a universal category of difference.[2] In Picart and Bernard's milieu, music and religion were categories of difference that became objects of fascination, knowledge, and profit. Their (largely) sympathetic, encyclopedic project focused readers' imaginations on religious rituals and practices rather than belief, theology, or the active presence of other-than-human beings. More than two centuries on, a disentangled ethnomusicology would share that focus.

Religious Ceremonies of the World differs from other direct and compiled accounts of imperial, colonial, and missionary encounter commonly invoked to represent ethnomusicology's fraught origins: Jean de Léry's *History of a Journey Made Into the Land of Brazil* (1580), Juan de Torquemada's *Monarquía indiana* (1615), John Scheffer's *The History of Lapland* (1673), Jean-Jacques Rousseau's

Music and Religion. Jeffers Engelhardt, Oxford University Press.
 DOI: 10.1093/9780190699185.003.0002

Figure 1.1 *Tableau des principales religions du monde*, frontispiece from Bernard and Picart's *Cérémonies et coutumes religieuses de tous les peuples du monde*, volume 1 (1727). Picart's engraving to open the first volume reflects the project's sympathetic, encyclopedic aims. "Idolatrous" people from beyond Europe are in the background, yet still part of a common

Figure 1.1 Continued

world of religions described in the caption. In the foreground, Muslims (backs turned to the drama behind them), Jews, Catholics, and Orthodox Christians (among others) are fazed by a female figure and notable Protestant Reformers at the left. The female figure gestures with her right hand to the Bible and has pruned the dead branches of the tree of religion, at whose roots another woman is baptized. (© The Trustees of the British Museum 1895,1015.87)

Dictionnaire de musique (1768), Charles Burney's *A General History of Music* (1776–1789), Jean Joseph Marie Amiot's *Mémoire sur la musique des Chinois* (1779), or Sir William Jones's *On the Musical Modes of the Hindus* (1792), for instance. In de Léry, Tupinambá shamans (*caraïbes*) use *maracas* to "bamboozle" idolatrous others into hearing "spirits speak" and providing the sacred instruments with food and drink (Harrison 1973: 23). In de Torquemada, indigenous officiants in New Spain "began their incense-offering and sacrifice and lauds and praises of the Devil" with the "music of horns and drums" (1973: 40). And in Scheffer, the Sámi shaman drum (*kannus*) reveals how the devil "stifles the faculties of the soul for a time" (1973: 81) in the shamanic journey. In these cases, others' sacred sonic practices are cast into the realm of superstition, witchcraft, or devil worship. They are absolutely other to these writers' Christianity and humanity and are positioned outside a shared space of comparable world religions.[3]

Rather than serve an agenda of dehumanization and domination, however, Picart and Bernard fashion a shared space of comparable world religions and comparable sacred musical practices. Through their visualization and audiation of assembled descriptions, Picart and Bernard encountered the shock of sameness that came through the disruption of Eurological, Christian-centric thinking. As French Protestants working in early-1700s Amsterdam, Picart and Bernard struck a balance in their secular project, espousing an anti-anti-Semitism in their approach to Judaism, a delicate touch with the Catholicism they distanced themselves from, judiciousness in the loaded task of "rehabilitating" Islam, and intrepidity in taking seriously and on equal terms the religion of "heathens" and "idolators"

(Hunt, Jacob, and Mijnhardt 2010a). At the outset of the first volume of *Religious Ceremonies of the World* dedicated to "the ceremonies and religious customs of the Jews and the Roman Catholicks" and based off of earlier writing by the Swiss Hebraist Johannes Buxtorf (1564–1629) and the Venetian rabbi and poet Leon (Judah Aryeh) Modena (1571–1648), Picart and Bernard present the possibility of comparing religions through practice:

> Were we to enlarge on the Topick of religious Kisses, on the Hymns, and sacred Dances performed in Honour of the Deity, three capital Points in ceremonious Religion, we might there find Matter enough for a complete Dissertation. We shall therefore say as little of them as possibly we can. [For the ancients,] it was customary to salute the Hands, and often the very Mouths of the Gods. It likewise was usual to kiss their Feet and Knees: in short, it was a part of Devotion to kiss the Doors of the Temples, the Pillars and Posts of the Gates, the Ground of any foreign Country on their first Arrival; and indeed, what would they not have kissed? since it was sufficient, for the Extravagance of Superstition, to find out any odd and fantastical Object, to persuade Mankind to have Confidence in and rely upon it. It is from a Superstition of the like Nature, that the *Turks* and other Mahometans, who go in Pilgrimage to *Mecca*, kiss the black Stone which they call *Hagiar Alasuad*, and the four Corners of the *Kaba*. The modern Idolaters in the *East Indies* and *America* observe likewise that Part of the religious Worship which the *Roman* Catholicks have consecrated in Honour of the Cross, and Relicks of Saints; the latter have likewise consecrated it on Occasions of Ceremony; as in the sprinkling of holy Water, the Priest kisses the *Aspergillum*, or holy Water-stick; and at the Procession on Palm-Sunday, the Deacon kisses the Palm which he presents to the Priest. It would be tedious, if not impertinent, to enlarge upon this Subject, or to be particular as to the Time and Manner of the Priest's kissing the Altar, of the Kisses bestowed on the Incensory, Patin, and Chalice, the white Stole, the Priest's Hand, &c. When People could not with any Convenience kiss the Object of their Devotion, they used to kiss their own Hands, and so throw up Kisses to the Gods. This religious Practice is daily observed amongst the *Spaniards* and *Portuguese*, who cross their

> Thumb with the Fore-Finger, and kiss their Hand afterwards in Honour of any distant Image. (1733–1739 vol. 1:19–20)

While taking a swipe at Roman Catholicism by likening its material and embodied devotion to idolatry, the Protestants Picart and Bernard were guided by anti-orthodox egalitarianism throughout *Religious Ceremonies of the World*, particularly in the sixth volume's treatment of deism and atheism. Their comparative approach "showed how all religions, even heathen idolatry, shared certain common human qualities—a concern with birth, marriage and death; a penchant for processions; a need for gods" (Hunt and Jacob 2010b: 3). This kind of comparison, sympathetic to difference with description stopping short of moral judgment, can be read as a secular proto-ethnomusicology that, in disentangling music and religion, distinguishes itself from sacred musicologies and sonic theologies.

Picart and Bernard's comparison has the effect of producing conjectural universals that unsettle some of the Eurological thinking they respond to. In the third volume of *Religious Ceremonies of the World*, Bernard notes that "the Singing of the *Americans*, which, though it be altogether rude and artless, is yet applied to the same Use as the rest of the World make of it, *viz.* that of praising their Gods, and their great Men, in diverting themselves, and regulating the Steps in their Dances" (1733–1739 vol. 3: 39). From this comparison, Bernard asks rhetorically (and, anachronistically, in remarkably antiracist language): "But why should not the Savages have as great a Share of this Frenzy as ourselves? Are they formed in a different Manner from the Inhabitants of our Hemisphere? are not their Organs the same as ours? or is the Construction of their Brain different?" (1733–1739 vol. 3: 39).

Picart and Bernard's attention to comparison and conjectural universals (at the expense of defending religious orthodoxy) leads them toward a theory of human–divine interaction made available by disentangling music and religion. Later on in the third volume, Bernard writes:

> Might we not, in order to justify this extraordinary manner of consulting God, and to explain it in a natural Way, take the Liberty of

> advancing, that the mind is more apt to receive the Commands of the divine Being, and listens more attentively to his Voice, in these Seasons when it has less Communication as it were with the Body; or when the Body is less capable of setting such Objects before it, as may call off its Attention. All such Things as had the Power of throwing the Senses into a kind of Lethargy, or that took off their Attention from all those Objects which were capable of disturbing them, prepared the Minds of the Prophets for receiving the Spirit of God; and 'tis certain, that nothing was better adapted to that Purpose than Voices, Instruments, and all kinds of Music, whose Sounds suspend, as it were, all the Faculties of the Soul, and raise it to Extasy.
>
> 'Tis in this manner that the *Indian Faquirs* in question, employ Drums, Trumpets, and other musical Instruments, to rouze their Souls, and enable them the better to publish their pretended Prophecies, in an artificial or voluntary Extasy. We always meet with one of these, who seems to be inspired with a kind of Fury, the violent Agitations of whose Body correspond with the sudden and irregular Cadence of those Instruments. No sooner have they worked themselves out of Breath, but they pronounce certain Sentences, which the Heathens consider as so many Oracles and Prophecies. (1733–1739 vol. 3: 265–266)

For Bernard, the "natural way" of accounting for divine encounter and inspiration is through the musical attuning and entraining of the senses. Sound, in other words, narrows and intensifies the sensory field, opening channels for ecstatic experience across the world's religions. This holds true for the Hindu ascetics (*fakirs*) Bernard enlists (with his characteristic skepticism of ecstatic religious experience) as examples of his conjectural universal. Instrumental sound effects ritual transformations of consciousness in *fakirs*, who are able to communicate their knowledge of the divine after being away. In *Religious Ceremonies of the World*, we encounter music and religion disentangled in Picart and Bernard's encyclopedic comparative work—a secular, Enlightenment project moving away from sacred musicologies, sonic theologies, and moralistic critiques of non-Christian religions.

A Music/Religion/Secular Impasse

In telling the story of a disentangled ethnomusicology, I now leap from the eighteenth-century proto-ethnomusicological moment of Picart and Bernard's *Religious Ceremonies of the World,* across the object-oriented comparative and national musicology of the 1880s–1940s (e.g., Bartók, Ellis, Stumpf, Hornbostel, Sachs, Schneider, and Lachmann), to the advent of a culture-oriented ethnomusicology. David McAllester's *Enemy Way Music: A Study of Social and Esthetic Values as Seen in Navaho Music* (1954) is, as others have noted (Rice 2017: 26), an early outlier in ethnomusicology for naming religion as a sonic-social field and adopting the religion/secular binary that was commonplace in midcentury social sciences.

The Enemy Way (*Ana'í Ndáá'*) is a multi-day ceremony to overcome the harmful effects of non-Diné ghosts (*ch'į́įdii*) in symptomatic individuals. In *Enemy Way Music,* McAllester draws on 1950 fieldwork in Diné communities of the Navajo Nation in an attempt to disentangle music and religion in search of Diné aesthetic values: ideas about beauty and the good linked to qualities of voice and formal aspects of text, melody, and song genre.[4] By his own admission, McAllester's project is complicated (if not rendered impossible) by his "own cultural bias" (1954: 4) in seeking to disentangle "music," which did not have a Diné equivalent, and "religion," which was "not compartmentalized" in Diné worlds, meaning "*all* music is religious" (1954: 5). The religion/secular binary was an artifact of modern secularization theories made problematic through McAllester's work with Diné research participants. "Esthetic desiderata" associated with religious music "can be derived only from a musicological examination"; "they are not discussed as such" by Diné singers (1954: 5). The familiar comparative musicological transcriptions and taxonomies of pitch, scale, melodic contour (see Figure 1.2), and phrasing that take up most of the space in the first part of *Enemy Way Music* can be read as bringing public songs of the Enemy Way into legible categories of music and religion.

McAllester's comparative musicological moves reproduce categories alien to Diné singers, dancers, and listeners. Because McAllester only had access to the public aspects of the Enemy

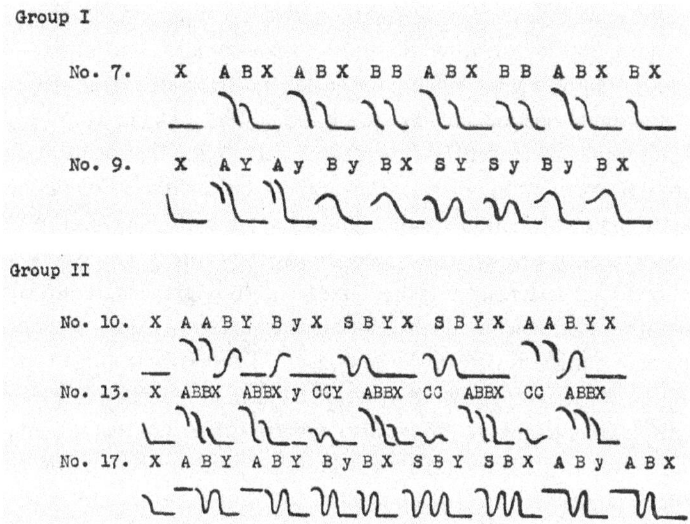

Figure 1.2 David McAllester's graphic representations (1954: 31–32) of characteristic sway song melodic profiles. (Peabody Museum Publications, Peabody Museum of Archaeology & Ethnology, Harvard University.)

Way, in which newly composed, ostensibly "secular" songs could be performed, and did not have access to "prayer ceremonials" performed and heard by those "properly protected by initiation" (1954: 63), his ideas about music and religion are filtered through his musicological categories and position in the field. The public sway songs, dance songs, gift songs, and circle dance songs in the Enemy Way are "the only ones that are also sung casually for entertainment in a secular context. They are the songs least freighted with overtones of magic, and it is therefore not surprising to find them different in form from the sacred songs. They are not chants but complex melodies" (1954: 25). The music-analytical complexity that McAllester's transcriptions and taxonomies could represent—melodies, not chants—was at odds with the "non-secular" Enemy Way songs he had no access to and, more broadly, with the larger questions of music and religion that occupied McAllester.

One of McAllester's key insights—indeed, an opening for what we now term ontological difference in ethnomusicological encounters—is that, for Diné singers, dancers, and listeners, "How does it sound"? is not the right question, but "What is it for?" (1954: 71). For McAllester, sound is the efficacy of Diné ceremonial, "a religion that seeks results through incantation" (1954: 71), and music analysis disentangled from religious function strains against the aims of his project in the second part of *Enemy Way Music*. In a section titled "The Nature of Taboo," McAllester suggests that Diné songs (the "prayer ceremonials" and other chants which he had little or no access to) do not *represent* power or danger but *are* power or danger: "There is no feeling that the singing of these songs by the wrong persons or at inappropriate times is displeasing to any supernatural persons or forces, but that the songs themselves are dangers" (1954: 64). Humans need protection from the potent dangers of song (much like they need protection from an electrical power line, in McAllester's analogy that was apt for his time), and this brings us to another of McAllester's key, implicit insights: songs are other-than-human agents that act in the world.

In *Enemy Way Music*, singers are bracketed off as mediators of song to make space for songs to enact their power. Humans become the "disappearing mediators" (Meyer 2011) that make it possible for McAllester to tacitly recognize other-than-human agency in Diné worlds. This is a subtle inversion of methodologically atheist and agnostic approaches to disentangling religion and social life through the phenomenological bracketing off of other-than-human agency from the real to distinguish postwar social science from theology. Rather than suspending judgment about the reality of gods, ghosts, and other-than-human agents to focus on the social facts of religious practice and belief, McAllester brackets off singers as mediators to focus on the danger songs are in Diné worlds. Although he stops short of explicitly admitting the other-than-human agency of songs into *Enemy Way Music*, McAllester's preoccupation with aesthetics is generative not of musicological and cultural certainties—he stresses throughout that "any neat separation of esthetics and religion" is not possible (1954: 5)—but of an encounter with songs' danger. At the end of part two, McAllester turns to the role of initiation, taboo, and right performance in guarding against the harms of songs' misuse. "Casual singing" (1954: 65) was not an option, and McAllester's "esthetic values" are ways of knowing about protection, misuse, and harm. His musicological categories (tonality, voice production, rhythm, tempo, and melodic line), in other words, are positions of knowing and using the powers of Diné song. Musical and ceremonial "mistakes" can expose patients and others to songs' potential harms.

McAllester's tacit, provisional recognition of songs' and other-than-human agency notwithstanding, he is committed in the designs of *Enemy Way Music* to disentangling music and religion to identify a Diné aesthetic. His is a culturalist ethnomusicology in which music is an object of study that exists in relationship with a religion/secular binary. That binary is the product of a cultural take on religion as a category of difference but, in a secular ethnomusicology, nothing more. Although McAllester describes his position alongside Diné research participants, he need not, in a disentangled, secular ethnomusicology, position himself relative to the powers and dangers of the Enemy Way songs he had access to. While McAllester does not reduce Enemy Way songs to their cultural functions, those songs and the other-than-human agents in Diné ceremony remain subjunctive aspects of culture against the real of musicological analysis, and this is his music/religion/secular impasse. McAllester's musical centering of "traditional" Enemy Way repertoires and singing styles chafes against his recognition that, for Diné singers, dancers, and listeners, music and religion are one thing (if those are even the right terms of the conversation). When McAllester notes changes in Enemy Way repertoires and singing styles, he attributes them to "the encroachment of white American culture and new religious ideas" (1954: 6), the advent of presentational singing styles (Turino 2008), and ideas of art for art's sake (1954: 71). These changes in the public Enemy Way songs McAllester was able to hear, divorced from Diné practices of receiving and adopting non-Diné songs, become proof of modern secularization theory rather than moments of generational adaptation or other-than-human agency. "It is my opinion," McAllester writes, "that the process of secularization is beginning to move up the scale of danger" from public songs and dances to the "prayer ceremonials" of male Enemy Way initiates (1954: 72). In *Enemy Way Music*, disentangling music and religion means that musical changes can happen apart from religious practice, reproducing a religion/secular binary that was, at best, weakly sensed in Diné worlds.

The Discipline of Disentangling

McAllester's commitment to holistic ethnographic fieldwork came to define culturalist ethnomusicology from the 1960s onward. Alongside systematic ethnomusicologies organized around scientific paradigms and the affordances of sound recording technologies (Lomax 1968; 1976), both the performance-oriented methods of Mantle Hood's "bi-musical" ethnomusicology (1960; 1971) and the anthropological orientation of Alan Merriam's ethnomusicology (1964) set about disentangling music and religion—a common feature across twentieth-century ethnomusicology's "great divide" (Pegg 2001) between the musical and the anthropological. Bi-musicality, as the name implies, centers on performed knowledge of music, perhaps distanced from its historical webs of meaning, use, and prohibition. The bi-musical ethnomusicologist can "sound" like an insider "without being one," adopted into community without claiming to know or represent others' musical experiences and sonic relationships (Titon 1995: 296). With regard to religion, the bi-musical ethnomusicologist need not convert or believe as others do; their performed abilities within a style are disentangled from relationships with other-than-human agency.

For Merriam's humanist, anthropologically oriented ethnomusicology, myths of other-than-human agency are simply a "warrant for human action" (Bialecki 2014: 43). Anthropology's methodological atheism from the 1960s onward meant that, according to Merriam, "men presuppose supernatural forces and powers which are related to and interested in men; and to communicate with these forces and powers there are men with special powers and abilities who serve as media between the human society and the supernatural world" (1961: 295). Ritual specialists' sonic mediation, in other words, can be disentangled as music from the supernatural worlds they performatively invoke through their address. Both ethnomusicological projects, then, bracket off religion and other-than-human agency in pursuit of secular, practice-based or social scientific knowledge.

A benefit of this moment was that in the decades-long process of ethnomusicology connecting musicological, ethnological, and folklore studies pedigrees, positivist comparative approaches, and culturalist ethnographic paradigms, disentangling music and religion meant clarifying what those categories actually were. Both music and religion were rethought in light of disciplinary developments that provincialized ethnomusicology's earlier use of those categories. From the 1960s into the 1980s, comparative work in anthropology and ethnomusicology on music and religion—work that necessarily broached the topic of analytically identifiable universals—exposed the limits of those categories through their reification. Edith Gerson-Kiwi (1961) and anthropologist Rodney Needham (1967), for instance, sought to generalize the role of voice and percussion, respectively, in religion. In "Religious Chant: A Pan-Asiatic Conception of Music," Gerson-Kiwi identified "the unnatural, non-human, spirit-like or godlike qualities of the human voice" (1961: 64) as a musical commonplace across the Asian landmass. She locates that voice in a variety of logogenic ("speech-melody"), melodically austere performances of sacred texts stylistically set apart from the "secular musics of their respective countries": "Shintoist, Buddhist, Brahman, Moslem and Hebrew sacred chant" (1961: 65). For Gerson-Kiwi, recitation around an axial pitch is a stylistic indication of religion as a category, "irrespective of [a style's] ethnic or religious origin" (1961: 67). Even as it reifies religion as a stylistically isolatable category, this approach does the work of refusing hierarchies of musicological value organized around aesthetic complexity. In Gerson-Kiwi's religious voice, other-than-human agency nearly finds space in ethnomusicology: when a singer performs a religious voice, "he is no longer himself; he represents a being of superhuman stature" (1961: 64).

In "Percussion and Transition," Needham sonically reifies religion (or what he ultimately frames as "transition") in addressing the naive question "why is noise that is produced by striking or shaking so widely used in order to communicate with the other world?" (1967: 606). While Needham's article is plagued by biased evaluative criteria ("noise") and unabashed speculation on "the bangs, thumps, taps, rattles, and other reverberations" and "universal psychic appeal of a certain kind of noise" (1967: 610), it represents an impulse to disentangle music and religion characteristic of Needham's moment and mode of scholarship. Indeed, Needham recognizes the pitfalls of universal comparison based on his conviction that "there is certainly no intrinsic relationship between the phenomena [of percussion and transition], yet the association is too firm for the answer to be sought in the contingent particulars of cultural tradition" (1967: 611). Needham's structuralism meant that disentangling musical artifacts and religious rituals confuses categories, creating an impasse at the intersection of the sonic and the "other world" of other-than-human beings (the spirit realm of shamanic transition, in Needham's article):

> On the one hand the institutions (beating of drums, etc.) have been defined reductionally by physical criteria (sound-waves, neural responses) which have no social content, whereas on the other hand institutions (sacrifice, etc.) which are equally social have merely been classed together sociologically in a way which retains their social and contingent nature. (1967: 612)

One is justified in wondering just how far from Picart and Bernard's universalizing comparative approach Gerson-Kiwi and Needham have come. The methodological atheism that disentangles the sonic (vocal style and organology for Gerson-Kiwi and Needham, respectively) from religion reinforced ethnomusicology's focus on musical artifacts and the assigning of other-than-human agency to the world of theology.

This disciplinary habit continued into the 1980s with the comparative impulse to disentangle musical style and sonic qualities in the reification of religion. Lois Ibsen al Faruqi's "What Makes 'Religious Music' Religious?," preoccupied with finding stylistic answers, assumes that question "must have been asked, either explicitly or implicitly, for millennia" (1983: 21). In fact, al Faruqi's evidence better addresses the questions of what makes Christian and Islamic musics Christian and Islamic in the sacred musicologies of Johannes Cotto (12th century CE) and al-Ghazālī (11th century CE)—a different aim than reifying religion as a universal category. Al Faruqi cites general stylistic features of "Gregorian" chant and Qur'ānic recitation (logogenicism, melodic restraint, breath-based phrasing, vocal modesty, exclusively vocal) and links them to theories of emotion and meaning in music to point to an inherently "religious" style in some music (1983: 26). That style, epitomized by "Gregorian" chant and Qur'ānic recitation, can map onto an immanence/transcendence theological continuum across religions, with early Christian chant and Qur'ānic recitation eschewing worldliness in order to "draw the worshiper away from this world" (1983: 28).[5] Ultimately, al Faruqi is unable to navigate the secular impasse of linking musical styles to religion as a category. "Are there then any universals for 'religious' music?," al Faruqi asks, "Or must every tradition express itself in religious sound patterns of a totally unique idiom?" (1983: 30). Beholden to a methodology of style analysis, she is caught between "the perimeters of the 'universally religious' and the 'specifically religious' in music":

> The answers to such questions are still to be worked out in full; but from the study thus far made, certain principles have crystallized. Just as there are certain theological premises which different religious traditions hold in common, there must be some analogous musical characteristics which pertain to all of a large number of the examples of religious music. But these universal characteristics of religious music are limited since the common features in religious thought which they symbolize are few. (1983: 30)

In anthropology, Donald Tuzin shared al Faruqi's conviction that there "must" be a direct, iconic connection between religious experience, ritual expression, and sound (1984: 579). In "Miraculous Voices: The Auditory Experience of Numinous Objects," Tuzin proposes that "a species of natural sounds epitomized by the complex acoustics of thunder" are, across animal species,

> *intrinsically* mysterious and thus anxiety-arousing; that this sensation is humanly interpreted and its accompanying anxiety cognitively resolved by referring it to the mystery that is allegedly inherent in the supernatural realm; and that certain kinds of ritual sounds capitalize on this iconic resemblance by simultaneously mimicking, as it were, factual and artifactual mystery, thereby summoning the

> senses to bear witness to the noetic truth of the sound's religious meaning. (1984: 579)

As a case in point of Tuzin's idea that religious ideology creates sonic objects for aural mysteries (and channels that mystery through ritual instruments like bullroarers and drums), he cites ethnographic evidence from Ilahita Arapesh ritual in Papua New Guinea. "These sounds," Tuzin writes,

> are mysterious also to the men who produce them. The initiate discovers that the interpretation revealed to him, viz., that the sounds are man-made, *is inadequate* to the experience he continues to have upon hearing them. While the naive illusion is dispelled, something about the quality of the sound rededicates the initiate to the truth that the spirits *are* real, though invisible, and that the ritual sounds *are* their voices. The problem, then, is to identify this mysterious aural quality and to account for its biocultural effect. (1984: 580)

Tuzin's commitment to biological and psychological explanations in service of a holistic anthropology leads him to posit universals of "religious experience" and "aural simuli" based on proposed causal connections between infrasound and its perception through the vestibular system. Infrasound (subauditory vibration below 20 Hz), a characteristic quality of Tuzin's thunder-like, "uncanny," "disturbing" religious sound, triggers "religious experience" because of "the inability or lack of conditioning of the temporal cortex to process soundlike vibratory inputs which do not reach it along the normal auditory pathways" (1984: 586).[6] Tuzin's methodological atheism will not admit a flat ontology in which the spirit voices he writes about in the subjunctive are not "intercranial events" (1984: 584). Ilahita Arapesh bullroarers' "sounds are so weirdly disturbing, so arresting in the local auditory environment" Tuzin writes, "that one is sorely tempted to agree with believers who maintain, against all reason, including their own, that they are not of this world" (1984: 582). Tuzin does not yield to temptation, however: aural stimuli, he claims, "can trigger those neural mechanisms underlying the so-called religious experience" (1984: 582).

Characteristic of the ethnomusicological moment here, Tuzin's critic John Blacking, in a comment on the article, takes issue not with Tuzin's methodological atheism and universalizing aims, but with his casual biological and psychological inductions and blurred distinctions between behavior and action, sensation and experience:

> Theories of the mysterious effects of sound and music have been put forward for so many decades and with such frequency that it is no longer acceptable to present them as conjectures [. . .] The evidence that emerges again and again, and that challenges Tuzin's contention that it is the unheard sounds that trigger the experience, is that sounds affect human behavior and action as a result of the ways in which people make sense of them. (Blacking 1984: 590)

As with Needham, Gerson-Kiwi, and al Faruqi, the upside of Tuzin's universalizing comparative approach is that it clarifies the limits of music and religion as reified categories. Throughout, Tuzin writes in terms of the inclusive category of sound rather than the circumscribed "social fact" of music. And in anticipation of currents in twenty-first-century sound studies, Tuzin is careful to distinguish between the humanness of audible sound, the frequency ranges audible as sound to other species, and the effects of inaudible vibration on human beings. (Alas, Tuzin and others do not address the latent ableism of their theories of religious sound.) Tuzin is also quick to point out that "religion" is a fluid category in his writing, shifting between "conventionally Christian" (1984: 584) notions of ecstasy and joy and the fear, dread, and disquieting vulnerability of Ilahita Arapesh ritual.

At the end of the decade, Philip Bohlman troubled conventional, universalizing associations of music and religion in the history of ethnomusicology. His provocation—"Is All Music Religious?" (1994 [1989])—is not a call for a nonsecular ethnomusicology but, rather, marks a moment for taking stock of the field as approaches to religion and other-than-human sonic agency were transforming. Responding to ethnomusicological work examining culturally specific (e.g., McAllester) and potentially universal (e.g., Needham, Gerson-Kiwi, al Faruqi, and Tuzin) characteristics of religious music and sound, Bohlman advocates for "a common ethnomusicological language about music and religion" formed around the ordinariness of religious sounds' ontological difference (1994 [1989]: 7). Bohlman's shift from musical analysis—what an ethnomusicologist hears—to sacred musicologies, sonic theologies, and ethnographic accounts of sonic relationships among human and other-than-human beings is a noteworthy moment of articulation in the field. For instance, a non-Muslim may hear Qur'ānic recitation or the *'adhān* (call to prayer) as "music" (and make generalizations about religious voice), but, as Bohlman emphasizes, Qur'ānic recitation and the 'adhān are not considered "music" in traditions of Islamic jurisprudence. They are ontologically distinct—divine revelation, in the case of the Qur'ān—and musical criteria do not fully speak to this ontological difference. "We might carefully analyze the recitation of a chapter from the Qur'an," Bohlman writes,

> observing the subtle ways in which pitch distinctions enhance the meaning of the text and pointing out the careful use of melodic modes, a use that could only result from years of careful study and practice, but the reciter would tell us that we are wasting our time on issues that have no relevance to the meaning of the recitation. The meaning is, of course, more profound and more fundamental than the aesthetic abstractions of the music. The meaning is the word of God, of 'Allah, revealed to us through the prophet Muhammad, embodied by the Qur'an, and expressed through the oral recitation of the text preserved in the Qur'an. (1994 [1989]: 8)

The other turn Bohlman marks is "the conflation of the religious with the ethnic or communal" (1994 [1989]: 9).[7] Purportedly secular repertoires and organizations are structurally dependent on religious institutions—Japanese *taiko* ensembles and Buddhist temples in the United States, for instance—while religious repertoires and practices may serve as cornerstones of ethnic identities—the sacred hymnody of German-American communities in northern Wisconsin, for instance. These flows between what can pass as religious and secular, an outcome of historical investments in reifying those categories, belie the slipperiness of those categories in a secular ethnomusicology. While Bohlman does not describe a nonsecular ethnomusicology that might move beyond methodological atheism, agnosticism, or ludism, he pithily expresses the stakes for an ethnomusicology of religion: "Identifying the presence of the religious in music would seem, in fact, to challenge the usual categories and constructs with which we commonly interpret music" (1994 [1989]: 11). Here, Bohlman turns ethnomusicology away from its comparative preoccupations with universally religious styles toward the implications of the religious in ethnomusicology, including the possibility of accounting for other-than-human agency.

Secular Ethnomusicology's Central Debates

The disentangling of music and religion I document here was at the center of productive ethnomusicological debates into the 1990s. Music, ethnomusicology's central object, category, and practice, was subject to increasing scrutiny from scholars of and within Muslim[8] and Buddhist[9] traditions who draw legal and doctrinal distinctions between categories of music and sacred sound. In other ethnomusicological work on sound, ritual, and other-than-human relationships, categories like song, prayer, dance, and drumming substitute for music for reasons of ethnographic representation rather than religious ideology.[10] So while the rise of music and religion in area studies, diasporic, and globalizing frames was a notable trend in ethnomusicology's growing interest in religion into the 1990s (e.g., Sullivan 1997), and the music half of that conceptual pair was critiqued in light of religious ontologies, doctrines, and practices, the religion half of that pair was subject to less scrutiny, remaining a taken-for-granted, culturalized, post-Enlightenment category of sonic experience and scholarly inquiry within the "music and identity episteme" (Sykes 2018: 4) that shaped music studies in the 1990s. One should also note that, as was the case with anthropology, Christianity, because of its close proximity to ethnomusicology's disciplinary, geographic, racialized, and epistemological genealogies, was far less present in the field—perhaps not "other" enough for ethnomusicology's representational and political commitments at the time.[11]

Here, I turn to two signature debates in ethnomusicology's disentangling of music and religion—the "problem" of trance and the "samā' polemic." In both debates, ethnomusicology continued to transform itself at its epistemological and categorical limits. In addition to terminology, the problem of trance, ecstasy, possession, and altered states of consciousness is, in a secular ethnomusicology, accounting for the sonic effects of other-than-human agency rather than the transitive power of musical qualities. The cause of trance, in other words, could not be fully attributed to analytically identifiable sonic details or human psychology, and taking trance seriously entailed the problem of subscribing to its unverifiable conditions, accounting for other-than-human agency, or reducing trance to culture.

In *The Soul of Mbira: Music and Traditions of the Shona People of Zimbabwe* (1978), Paul Berliner negotiates the problem with a functionalist approach to ancestral spirit possession in *bira* ritual. "Shona religious ritual," Berliner writes in a chapter on music and spirit possession, "rather than seeking to analyze statements of ideology, acts them out" (1978: 205). Berliner's focus on performative ritual does not require him to assess the veracity of spirit possession, although his ethnographic stance is one of measured skepticism (note the scare quotes) that typifies a secular ethnomusicology:

> At one ceremony I attended, a participant became possessed and began playing the *hosho* [gourd rattles] with a vengeance. As he played, his rattles temporarily overpowered the sounds of the mbira [Shona lamellophone] and everyone present was swept away by his "spirit's" powerful performance. As long as he was possessed, the participant's behavior followed the same pattern: he stood dancing and playing *hosho* furiously, expending every ounce of energy and strength until he fell exhausted to the ground. After catching his breath again, he rose to his feet and, still gasping for air, he resumed his performance with the same intensity. It was interesting to note that although the spirit's presence was exhilarating to the guests, the musicians complained about him the next day. He was playing *hosho* poorly; he was not following the rhythm of the mbira, and he could not keep a steady tempo. His presence was offensive and disruptive to their music. (1978: 196)

In reflecting on this sonic-ritual moment, Berliner isolates the social and scholarly problem of spirit possession: "When I asked the musicians if he was really to blame, they shrugged their shoulders: when a man is possessed by the spirit, he must follow the spirit's will—there was nothing he could do. This fact, however, did not fully compensate for their annoyance regarding the evening's performance" (1978: 196). As Berliner relates, Shona musicians accommodated other-than-human agency, even when it was musically disruptive. For Berliner, however, the move of emphasizing their "annoyance" leaves open the possibility that spirit possession is performative as well as "authentic" (1978: 201).

The problem of trance pinpointed ethnomusicology's shifting relationship with other-than-human agency, the analysis of musical objects and experiences, and tensions between relativism and universality. Gilbert Rouget's *Music and Trance: A Theory of the Relations between Music and Possession* (the 1980 French original translated into English in 1985) was a major inflection point in the discipline, working to dispel singular, universal notions of what trance, ecstasy, and possession are and disassociating musical style and formal characteristics from triggering and maintaining trance. "There are as many different kinds of possession music," Rouget writes, "as there are different possession cults" (1985: 73). Unlike Needham, Gerson-Kiwi, al Faruqi, and Tuzin, Rouget forecloses the possibility of universally religious sound—trance-triggering and trance-maintaining music, in this case.

Through a litany of case studies from the Orisha and vodun Black Atlantic worlds, the Arab Muslim world, ancient Greece, opera in the European Renaissance, and South American and Central Asian shamanism (a collection whose breadth draws attention to all that Rouget unapologetically excludes, including popular musics), Rouget systematically distinguishes trance (noise, movement, crisis) from ecstasy (silence, immobility, no crisis); shamanism ("acting") from possession ("undergoing"); and induced trance (participants are "musicated" into trance) from conducted trance (participants "musicate" themselves into trance). Although Rouget does recognize fluidity between these structural binaries, their main purpose is to underscore the non-universality of trance musics—a first step in addressing the problem of trance in ethnomusicology's secular epistemologies. For Rouget, the problem is compounded by the "disconcerting variability of the relation between music and the onset of trance" (1985: 323). "Although music indisputably plays a role—more or less decisive depending on the case—in the onset of trance," Rouget writes, "it seems impossible to establish any constant relation of cause and effect between the two" (1985: 322).[12]

While Rouget's resigned tone may be a response to the disciplinary prestige of comparative musical universals disentangled from religion, his defense of relativism articulates the main claim in *Music and Trance*, namely that music "socializes" trance; it "authenticates the trance and confers upon it a character of normality" (1985: 323). Trance, for Rouget, is "theatrical" in that it would be "meaningless if it were not recognized by the group" (1985: 325) (hence his exclusion of solitary trancing in the book).[13] Although the particulars of Rouget's assembled examples and terminological slippages strain under the generality of his theory, music's socializing of trance happens as melodies, rhythms, and mottos, collectively identified with spirits and divinities, affirm the "hysteriform behavior" of the trancer as "a sign of the will or presence" of an other-than-human being (1985: 322). The socialized theater of trance is a space that offers participants sonic scripts for volitional action, since they "have made the decisions (more or less unconsciously) to succumb to the trance state" (1985: 321).

Throughout *Music and Trance*, Rouget remains agnostic about the agency of other-than-human beings in trance. Although the book contains a separate index for "religions, sects, divinities, and religious figures," and Rouget writes easily about musicians', listeners', and trancers' relationships with spirits and divinities in everyday life (e.g., 1985: 123–124), his theory of the musical socialization of trancing does not admit other-than-human agency. Indeed, throughout *Music and Trance*, Rouget writes of "demystifying" (1985: xviii) the "illusion" (1985: 324) of music's causal, transitive power in triggering and maintaining trance, possession, ecstasy, and altered states of consciousness. When, for Rouget, sound is "of" a spirit or divinity, that "of" is the socialized link to systems of ideology and representation rather than sound that, in a flat ontology, is a channel of other-than-human agency.

In a lengthy chapter on Sufism in *Music and Trance*, Rouget also weighs in on the "samā' polemic" that occupied an important place in the ethnomusicology of music and religion into the 1990s. Rouget focuses his discussion on Abū Ḥāmid Muḥammad al-Ghazālī's 12th-century CE *Iḥyā' 'ulūm al-dīn (The Revival of the Religious Sciences)*, the eighth part of which ("Book of the Right Usages of Audition and Trance") justifies the Sufi practice of samā' (audition). Samā', for Rouget, is "the category of the objects of audition" (1985: 257) that are morally justified in Sufi practice: Qur'ānic recitation, poetry, and accompanied song. Rouget emphasizes al-Ghazālī's focus on the "inner purity" of the listener rather than the qualities of voice and music or the status of musicians and repertoires: "Heard with a pure heart, music can be lawful even though it would not be if one listened to it in a lascivious state of mind" (1985: 257). For ethnomusicology, this is a critical shift of perspective away from the qualities, aesthetics, and meanings of sonic objects (a commonplace throughout the discipline's history) toward the agency of listeners, ritual participants, and relationships with Sufi saints and God. Contextualized listening—the ecstasy of samā'—moved to the center of ethnomusicology and created space for encountering music as an effect of religion, not only as a cause.[14] This, in turn, placed greater strain on a secular ethnomusicology that assigned sonic agency exclusively to human musicians.

Ethnomusicologists and other scholars writing on the "samā' polemic" in the 1980s and 1990s[15] were returning to a longstanding discourse in Islamic law, theology, and mysticism that had already occupied music scholars for decades (e.g., Farmer 1952; Qureshi 1972). In brief, the polemic concerns the permissibility of "music" and audition in Islamic law and tradition and the moral status of musicians and listeners. Interpretations of Islamic sources (the Qur'ān and the *ḥadīth* literature) on the permissibility of samā' often function as ciphers of broader religious and political ideologies: "From the very beginning of Islamic history, therefore," writes Islamic scholar Seyyed Hossein Nasr, "the question of music and its legal status has been surrounded by an aura of ambiguity, which, in fact, has been a positive rather than a negative aspect of Islamic Law" (1997: 219).[16] This ambiguity stems from the absence of any explicit reference to "music" in the Qur'ān. The Qur'ān addresses *ghinā'* (sung poetry), but not the Greek-derived *mūsīqā* (borrowed in the 8th–10th centuries CE), which described rules for cultivating music as a secular art, not as a category of sound easily equated with the English-language concept of music (and its analogs in other languages).[17] Expressions seeming musical to an ethnomusicological ear are, in an Islamic frame, categorically not music. They are, for instance, Qur'ānic recitation (*quirā'ah*), the call to prayer ('adhān), or the ecstatic remembrance of God's names (*dhikr*). Absent clear Qur'ānic guidance on the obligatory or impermissible nature of musical audition, both sides in the "samā' polemic" had to select their evidence carefully. Opponents obliquely aligned music and its audition with Qur'ānic criticism of "diverting talk" (31: 5), poets' errancy (26: 224–226), sport and amusement (23: 1–3; 53: 64), Satan's voice (17: 64), and the sounds of idolaters (8: 35).[18] Proponents pointed to Qur'ānic praise of listening to a beautiful voice (35: 1; 39: 17–18) and the absence of an explicit prohibition on musical audition (6: 119) as justification for its permissibility.[19] Given the paucity of Qur'ānic guidance, the heart of the "samā' polemic" (and the focus of ethnomusicological scholarship in this moment) was in commentaries and interpretations of the ḥadīth literature, ranging from ibn Taymiyya's 14th-century CE condemnation of samā' as "infidel and polytheist" (Shiloah 1995: 35) to al-Ghazālī's measured praise of musical audition.

The availability of centuries of discourse on the (im)permissibility of audition and music in Islam offered scholars opportunities to bring listener-centered, ethically oriented methodologies into ethnomusicology. Engaging the "samā' polemic" placed human relationships with God, shaped by Islamic law and tradition, at the center of ethnomusicological knowing rather than incidental to it, and, unsurprisingly, these authors are ideologically sympathetic to the permissibility of audition and music in Islam. Kristina Nelson, for instance, describes a listener-centered, ethically oriented position: "Music is itself a neutral, if potent, power; it is the spiritual state of the listener that transforms its influence into a tool for good or evil" (1985: 45). And later: "Music is a neutral force which, channeled and regulated, can just as well lead to God as away from Him" (1985: 50). Through the "samā' polemic," the reality and nature of relationships between human beings and God became a premise of ethnomusicology and a key feature of what some celebrated as a proto-decolonizing "Islamic ethnomusicology."[20]

Another key ethnomusicological concern articulated in the "samā' polemic" was the question of music and ontological relativism. Al Faruqi's often-reproduced hierarchy of "sound art expressions" (*handasah al-ṣawt*), shown in Figure 1.3, represents Islamic ontologies of voice, sound, and music. These descend from the most legitimate (*ḥalāl*) forms of "non-music" bound to required practices (Qur'ānic recitation, the call to prayer), through "controversial" forms of vocal and instrumental "sound art" deemed "music" and ambivalently associated with Islamic contexts of audition, to illegitimate (*ḥarām*) music associated with un-Islamic contexts of audition.[21] While the ḥalāl/ḥarām continuum of al Faruqi's table is historically, ideologically, and culturally fluid (a fact al Faruqi's critics claim is overlooked in her essentialist rendering), it represents an abstract relationship between Islamic contexts of audition and sonic ontologies, which al Faruqi's contemporaries documented in more granular ethnographic detail (e.g., Sakata 1983; Slobin 1976).

The "samā' polemic" fits awkwardly into ethnomusicology's story of disentangling music and religion precisely because it unsettled some of ethnomusicology's cherished models. To be sure, the pair Islam and music perpetuate the reification and disentangling of those categories, but the appeal of the "samā' polemic" for ethnomusicologists in the 1980s and 1990s was that it calibrated ethnomusicological ways of knowing around an ontological relativism rooted in Islamic discourse. As a "foreign science" (Sakata 1983: 40), mūsīqā as the object of ethnomusicology could not encompass the sounds of Islam. The disentangling of music and religion, in other words, amplified ethnomusicology's epistemological limits.

The "samā' polemic" also troubled the bracketing off of other-than-human agency in a disentangled, secular ethnomusicology. If, in a centrist assessment of the permissibility of samā', music and sound are neutral forces, then the relationship of listeners to God becomes crucial in legitimizing samā'. Islamic studies scholar Leonard Lewisohn, drawing on the Persian Sufi polymaths al-Ghazālī and Naṣīr al-Dīn al-Ṭūsī, emphasizes that there is a "right time," "right place," and "right company" for "reverently listening to music" (1997: 4). Glossing al-Ghazālī's and al-Ṭūsī's writing on Sufi mysticism, Lewisohn positions samā' in an esoteric "psychological, liturgical, and sociological

Table: HIERARCHY OF
HANDASAH AL ṢAWT GENRES

	Qur'ānic Chant (qirā'ah)	
NON-MŪSĪQĀ	Religious Chants (adhān, tahlīl/talbiyyah, takbīrāt, madīḥ, tasbīḥ, and taḥmīd)	
	Chanted Poetry with noble themes (shi'r)	LEGITIMATE
	Family/Celebration Music (lullabies, women's songs, wedding songs, etc.)	(ḤALĀL)
	"Occupational" Music (caravan chants, shepherd's tunes, work songs, etc.)	
	Military Music (Ṭabl Khānah)	
MŪSĪQĀ	Vocal/Instrumental Improvisations (layālī, āvāz, taqāsīm, istikhbār, etc.)	
	Serious Metered Songs (dawr, muwashshaḥ, taṣnīf, etc.) & Instrumental Music (bashraf, dā'irah, samā'ī, dūlāb, etc.)	Controversial (ḤALĀL, MUBĀḤ, MAKRŪH, ḤARĀM)
	Music Related to Pre-Islamic or Non-Islamic Origins	
	Sensuous Music Associated with Unacceptable Contexts	ILLEGITIMATE (ḤARĀM)

Figure 1.3 Lois Ibsen al Faruqi's (1985: 8) hierarchy of "sound art expressions" (*handasah al-ṣawt*). (© The University of Texas Press. Reproduced with permission.)

substructure" (1997: 12) that cultivates and ensures its efficacy. For Lewisohn, an ethnomusicological understanding of samā' begins with auditors' "right" spiritual conditions in relationship to God—a sonified relational ontology in line with a Sufi "eros" doctrine of the soul's divinity (Gribetz 1991: 52).

For those opposed to samā', the relationship of humans and God in audition blurs the "mutual exclusivity of the divine and human spheres" (Nelson 1985: 49). In line with a legalist "nomos" doctrine of the complete dissimilarity of God and humans (Gribetz 1991: 55), the experience of samā' in its more musical forms confuses human artifice for knowledge of God, and ethnomusicologists seeking to understand this position must move auditors' agency further to the margins of Islamic sound. This take on the "samā' polemic" lingers at the very top of al Faruqi's hierarchy of sound art expressions where the human voice is a tightly controlled mediator of divine agency, "bearer and servant of the message contained in the text" (Shiloah 1995: 37). To come to terms with centrists' and opponents' positions in the "samā' polemic," then, ethnomusicologists had to account for the reality of other-than-human agency in Islamic sound and audition or risk leveling the difference of Islamic theologies and ontologies in the discipline.

Into the 1990s, ethnomusicologists' encounters with the problem of trance and the "samā' polemic" demonstrated the enduring disciplinary practices of disentangling music and religion and limiting the extent of other-than-human agency in ethnomusicological knowing. At the same time, the problem of trance and the samā' polemic" exposed the limits of a secular ethnomusicology whose methods centered around universal categories (music, trance) and ahistorical generalizations (Islam, possession) rather than more granular ethnographic knowledge (the sounds and scenes of Rouget's socialization and the politics and positions of samā' apologists and critics, for instance).

Listening as Disentangling

It was into this space that Regula Burckhardt Qureshi stepped with her monumental *Sufi Music of India and Pakistan: Sound, Context, and*

Meaning in Qawwali, first published in 1986. Qureshi's study is a systematic, structuralist account of Qawwali performance, listening, and patronage at the Nizamuddin Auliya shrine (*dargah*) in New Delhi. The book moves readers from the poetic forms and Hindustani musical traditions that define Qawwali as a religious genre, through the saintly genealogies and social hierarchies that shape Qawwali performance at the Nizamuddin Auliya shrine, to detailed transcriptions of the micro-interactions between Qawwali musicians and ecstatic listeners that constitute the experience of mystical listening, or samā'. Qureshi's positioning and methodology in *Sufi Music of India and Pakistan* are agnostic. She was "part of the scene as a listener and recorder of every Qawwali event, a seeker of Sufi knowledge, a student of Qawwali performers; I was also the wife of a respected patron from abroad—a foreigner but also an insider" who received "the hospitality of India and Pakistan's Sufi saints, extended to me most generously by their descendants and their affiliated performers" (Qureshi 1995: xv; see 12–13 for more on her positioning).

Qureshi's accomplishment of reconciling the sonic and the social—"the musical sound structure" and "the structure of the performance occasion" (1995: xiv)—characterized an ethnomusicological moment focused on "sound structure as social structure" (Feld 1984) and the productive disentangling of music and religion. In answering the guiding question of "How does Qawwali, the music, articulate with Qawwali, its context of performance?," (Qureshi 1995: 5), Qureshi works expertly within a secular ethnomusicology's epistemological limits. "With the Sufi," she writes, "we must accept the mystery of the samā' experience, the ultimate Why; yet it is possible to pursue the How" (1995: 133). The how, for Qureshi, is "what can be tested, the observable" in "making structure operational" (1995: 10).

Qawwali is the professional performance of mystical Sufi poetry in Farsi, Hindi, and Urdu. Strophic tunes are performed through call-and-response and solo vocal improvisations, accompanied by the barrel-shaped *dholak* drum, handclapping, and the harmonium. At the shrine to the 13th-century CE Sufi saint Nizamuddin Auliya, the musicians of the Qawwal Bachche, led by Qureshi's principal teacher Meraj Ahmad, performed a repertoire centering on the compositions of Amir Khusrau, the 13th-century CE Sufi poet, Nizamuddin Auliya disciple, and "father of Qawwali" whose tomb is adjacent to the saint's. Qawwal Bachche claimed their descent from Khusrau (1995: 245) but occupied "a totally insignificant position" as "service professionals," despite having a "key function in the central ritual of Sufism": the *mahfil-e-samā'* (a gathering for listening) (1995: 96–97). These musicians' low status connects back to the "samā' polemic" and the spiritual advancement achieved through listening rather than musical performance (1995: 107–108). Along these lines, at Qawwali assemblies, listener seating is oriented around spiritual leaders and a saint's tomb, not around performers.

Nevertheless, Qawwali performers played an essential role in the mahfil-e-samā' by selecting repertoire suited to the moment and their patrons, responding to the listening practices of spiritual leaders, and fulfilling

> one principal requirement: to repeat or amplify any effective part of a song. This becomes crucial when a devotee attains a state of ecstasy; at that point it is incumbent upon the singers to repeat incessantly and briskly the particular song segment that inspired the state. (1995: 127)

The micro-interactional dynamics of lower-status Qawwali musicians and middle- or higher-status Qawwali listeners are central in Qureshi's analysis of Qawwali's spiritual and financial economy. On the one hand, a Qawwali musician's "financial success ultimately derives from 'scoring' at the spiritual level" (1995: 139). And on the other hand, "the only way to control the Qawwal's musical power over his audience is to give his audience religiously legitimized social and economic power over him" (1995: 231).

This brings us to the heart of *Sufi Music of India and Pakistan,* where Qureshi offers us meticulously rendered transcriptions of the musical and social micro-interactions that mediate individuals' experiences of mystical love (1995: 79) and the enduring hierarchies of institutionalized Sufism. In Figure 1.4, a reproduction of Qureshi's graphing of a short section of Khusrau's "Tōrī sūrat ke balhārī" ("Beholding your countenance I offer myself in sacrifice") from videotape, we encounter Qureshi's interpretation of Qawwali micro-interactions.

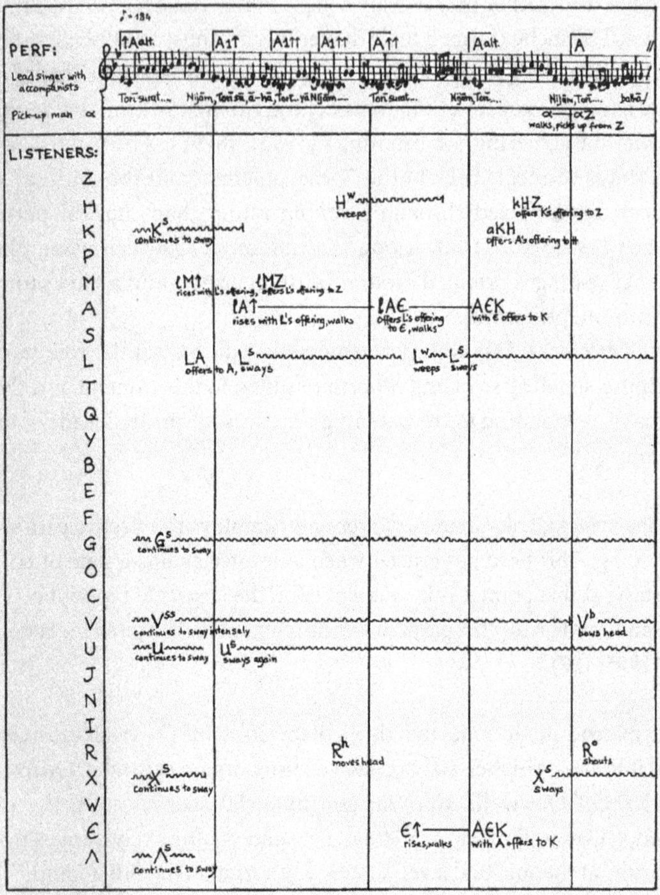

Figure 1.4 Regula Burckhardt Qureshi's transcription (1995: 169) of performer/listener micro-interactions in a section of "Tōrī sūrat ke balhārī." (© Cambridge University Press. Reproduced with permission of The Licensor through PLSclear.)

At the top of the graph, Meraj Ahmad repeats the Hindi refrain "Tōrī sūrat" with alternate tunes (A, A1, A alt.) and at elevated pitch levels (upward arrows) out of his awareness of "special listeners who are showing incipient arousal" (1995: 164; see 1995: 144–145 for a complete description of the assembled listeners and spiritual leaders). Listeners H, K, L, G, V, U, X, and Λ are swaying throughout (wavy lines); others (listeners H and L) weep; and still others rise to make offerings. When Meraj Ahmad realizes that the special listeners' spiritual arousal is not increasing in response to his improvised repetitions,

> he decides to insert a *girah* [inserted recitative verse, not yet appearing in Figure 1.4] to expand on the range of meaning inherent in the opening line. First, however, he waits for a prosperous devotee (Є) to complete his offering to the leader and for it to be passed up the hierarchy, to Khwaja Hasan Sani [K], the leader [of the Nizamuddin Auliya assembly], to Syed Haleem Chishti [H], the *gaḍḍīnashīn* [spiritual leader] of Ajmer [the location of the Muinuddin Chishti shrine], and finally to Zainul Abedin [Z], the *dīwān* [saint's successor] of Ajmer, so that his pick-up man [shown at the top of Figure 1.4 under Meraj Ahmad and his accompanists] can receive it and deposit it on the harmonium. (Qureshi 1995: 164)

In Figure 1.4, Qureshi graphs the moment-to-moment textual and vocal flow of Meraj Ahmad's performance decisions onto hierarchically positioned listeners' embodied expressions of spiritual arousal, Meraj Ahmad's failure to intensify that arousal, the circulation of monetary offerings that make their way up a spiritual hierarchy and become payment to Qawwali performers, and the structural constraints and possibilities of Khusrau's "Tōrī sūrat" in Qawwal Bachche's practice. Qureshi's graph is not linear, however, not least because of Meraj Ahmad's looping textual and melodic repetitions. To read from top to bottom makes Meraj Ahmad's performance decisions determinative of Qawwali's spiritual effects; to read from bottom to top makes listeners' actions determinative of Qawwali's musical form. Qureshi's graph demonstrates her key claim about the mahfil-e-samā': it enacts a feedback loop between the musical performance of Qawwali and the social occasion of Qawwali—top to bottom, bottom to top, and so on. Qureshi is able to represent the bootstrap dynamics of Qawwali performance and the Qawwali occasion in such micro-interactional detail thanks to her intimate knowledge of Qawwali repertoire and the religious world of the Nizamuddin Auliya shrine.

This inserted *Sufi Music of India and Pakistan* into contemporaneous conversations on language performance (Bauman 1975; Silverstein 1976), the poetics of religion (Dumont 1970; Geertz 1968), and theories of ritual (Bell 1992; Turner 1969) precisely because of Qureshi's approach to disentangling music and religion. Qawwali music (placed in its own box at the top of Qureshi's graph in Figure 1.4) is the "musicological" object of her study that articulates both the "ideology" and "social reality of Sufism," which pervades her graph in its entirety (Qureshi 1995: 228). The bootstrap dynamic Qureshi is able to pinpoint, then, is that "Qawwali music conveys to its listeners affirmation of traditional structures, whether ideological or social. It does so by its very dependence on those structures for successful articulation in performance" (1995: 228). But, crucial for Qureshi's interest in musical variability and change, Qawwali "contains within it a meaning contradictory to its own contextual framework" (1995: 228) due to Sufism's respect for individual spiritual experience. Meraj Ahmad or a low-status listener could, to an extent, transform Qawwali through their agency in the performance/listening feedback loop. By disentangling music and religion, Qureshi achieves her disciplinary intervention: musical sound, in the case of Qawwali, is the sounding of music's "contextual dimension" (1995: xiv) with the potential to transform that context.

At the same time, Qureshi's music/context distinction addressed a discipline in which the disentangling of music and religion, which can claim music as the purview of ethnomusicology, continued to rely on music and religion as culturalist forms of difference. This issue was not lost on Qureshi, who is aware of the potential pitfalls of centering music and musicians in a world where they are ideologically and socially marginal. Qureshi writes: "Has it then, in fact, been a fallacious Western premise of this analysis to focus on the artist as the agent of musical creativity and to consider him the catalyst of the musical event" (1995: 230)? In this moment, making one's work legible to the discipline meant disentangling music and religion to render both as knowable objects of study. In a secular ethnomusicology, Qureshi's emphasis on artists' and listeners' agency leaves unexamined (or unexaminable) other-than-human agency in the mahfil-e-samā' through the relationships of Sufi seekers, devotee listeners, sheikhs' disciples, and saints' successors with, in Sufi terms, the Beloved. Qureshi's poetic, evocative field notes, peppered throughout *Sufi Music of India and Pakistan*, give us an impression of how these relationships enter into Qawwali's feedback loops: "The singer's aim is always to move, to arouse, to draw the listener toward his Sheikh, the saint, to God, and into the ecstasy of mystical union" (1995: 4). And in the Qawwali texts Qureshi offers us throughout the book, other-than-human agency is celebrated in poetic fervor:

> I know not in what state and in what wondrous
> place I found myself last night
> Victims of Love ecstatic danced all around me
> where I found myself last night
>
> God Himself was Lord of this assembly—o
> Khusrau, partaker of the Infinite
> Muhammad was the Beloved illuminating that
> wondrous place where I found myself last night (1995: 133)

Setting *Sufi Music of India and Pakistan* aside, one wonders what Qawwali performers and listeners themselves know about the flows of spiritual arousal and musical variation they experience and create at a Qawwali assembly. Not doing secular ethnomusicology, might they communicate their knowledge with unselfconscious invocation of the Beloved in addition to an awareness of their status and role in a Qawwali assembly?

(Dis)entangling

Although this book may, at times, feel like a chronological story of ethnomusicological encounters with religion, it is not. At the intersections of the two central chapters of *Music and Religion*, the Venn diagram of ethnomusicology's secular disentangling and nonsecular entangling of music and religion overlaps. Indeed, the distinctions between disentangled and entangled ethnomusicologies are less hard and fast than I inevitably make them here. In my reading, disentangling music and religion is the norm in ethnomusicology (and music studies as a whole), and work on music and religion continues to thrive. As this chapter shows, the signal contribution of disentangling music and religion comes from centering sound within the ideological, aesthetic, and ritual forms of religion, and this part of the story is far from over.

Indeed, this strand of work on music and religion has bloomed in the twenty-first century. In Gregory Barz's *Performing Religion: Negotiating Past and Present in Kwaya Music of Tanzania* (2003), we are offered an ethnography of Lutheran singing communities (*kwayas*) in Dar es Salaam that reassesses colonial logics of missionary and indigenous Lutheran musicality. Barz disentangles music and religion to move "beyond syncretism toward consciousness" in encountering the textures of "European hymnody, Central African dance musics, and East African melodic and rhythmic elements" (2003: 2) in *kwaya* members' lives. In other work on the same subject, Barz demonstrates how disentangling Christian, Islamic, and "traditional African" religious elements serves a more general critical project. To show how kwaya consciousness moves beyond the derivative syncretism of those disentangled elements, Barz moves beyond the "naming of parts" (2006: 23) that characterizes much thinking on post-colonial Africa.

As a methodology, disentangling brings the promise of disrupting hardened associations of identities and sacred traditions that may mask more nuanced theological and historical understandings. In *Jewish Music and Modernity* (2008), Philip Bohlman interprets how sacred practices and social positions intersect and transform musically across histories, geographies, and the Holocaust in the making of modern Jewish identities. In disentangling music and religion, Bohlman unsettles the comfortable, fraught alignment of music and religion along the lines of belief, race, and ethnicity since, in Jewish musical modernity, Jews and non-Jews alike play key roles in the performance and representation of Jewishness in prayer, on stage, and in ethnomusicological scholarship.

As other recent work shows, naming the sounded associations of religions and identities that harden in the making of states, subjects, and citizens is an essential move. Rachel Harris's *Soundscapes of Uyghur Islam* (2020) is an urgent documentation of women's ritual practice and transnational media circuits in and through China's Xinjiang Uyghur Autonomous Region, where Uyghurs face "surveillance on an unprecedented scale and the mass detention of more than a million of the region's citizens" (2020: 203). Harris's disentangling of music and religion shows the affective power of Qur'ānic sound and digital media in the making of Uyghur Islam and the impacts of state-organized anti-religious extremism and forced re-education within a Muslim soundscape in Xinjiang. Zoe Sherinian's *Tamil Folk Music as Dalit Liberation Theology* (2014) approaches the musico-theological work of Rev. Dr. James Theophilus Appavoo in Tamil Nadu as a Christian response to Dalit oppression. Sherinian disentangles music and religion to situate indigenous musical forms and styles as media for class, gender, and caste liberation within the Protestant Church of South India. And in *Women, the Recited Qur'an, and Islamic Music in Indonesia* (2010), Anne Rasmussen offers us an ethnographic documentation of ongoing Islamization in Indonesia through its sonic atmospheres. Rasmussen's disentangling of music and religion creates space for a corrective account of women's roles in Islamic musical arts (and, therefore, the permissibility of Islamic music in Indonesia) and in transmitting the prestige associated with Egyptian Qur'ānic recitation as reciters and teachers.

Finally, disentangling creates space for a sustained focus on musical aesthetics. Mark Kligman's *Maqām and Liturgy: Ritual, Music, and Aesthetics of Syrian Jews in Brooklyn* (2009) is an account of a Judeo-Arab synthesis in Syrian Jewish liturgical performance. By taking up Syrian Jews' use of *maqām* (the modal system of Arab music), Kligman disentangles music and religion as an "Arab aesthetic" and "Jewish life" (2009: 166) to analyze the affective and imaginative associations guiding the pairing of a maqām with a specific liturgical text and the transformations of a maqām that pairing effects. Similarly, Christopher Witulski's *The Gnawa Lions: Authenticity and Opportunity in Moroccan Ritual Music* (2018) listens to the braiding of ritual music and ritual economy in the performance of Muslim piety and sub-Saharan identity. To understand the contingencies of *gnawa* authenticity, Witulski disentangles music and religion to hold sub-Saharan musical practices, Islam, and performers' abilities to please clients, audiences, trancing bodies, and spirits in productive tension.

Now I pivot to the next chapter, where I read and listen across the overlaps of disentangled and entangled ethnomusicologies from another vantage. Building off of and in conversation with the disciplinary touchstones I write about here, the entangled ethnomusicology I turn to in the next chapter, no longer emergent but not yet commonplace, is the outcome of ethnomusicology's embrace of nonsecular engagements with theology, other-than-human agency, and a multiplicity of scholarly positionalities. Rather than documenting a rupture within the field, however, I encounter nonsecular ethnomusicologies in the next chapter as resurgent practices that were once forgotten, abandoned, and excluded from the discipline.

Notes

1. The project was originally published as *Cérémonies et coutumes religieuses de tous les peuples du monde* in 1723–1737.
2. In their meditation on *Religious Ceremonies of the World*, Lynn Hunt, Margaret Jacob, and Wijnand Mijnhardt observe that "this global survey of religious practices effectively disaggregated and delimited the sacred, making it specific to time, place, and institutions. Once labeled in time and place, religion became not an unchanging system of beliefs but a discrete entity concerned everywhere with the gods or the heavenly" (2010a: 2).
3. Cf. Anna María Ochoa Gautier (2014) on the recognition of humanness and personhood in colonial sonic encounters in South America and the Caribbean.
4. For a perspective on McAllester's work in the context of value theory in ethnomusicology, see Timothy Taylor's insightful discussion of *Enemy Way Music* in *Making Value: Music, Capital, and the Social* (2024: 5–10).
5. Philip Bohlman and I explore slippages in the immanence/transcendence binary in our introduction to *Resounding Transcendence: Transitions in Music, Religion, and Ritual* (2016). Also see Sahlins (2022) for a further decoupling of immanence and secularity.
6. Robert Fink provides us with a nuanced corrective to Tuzin-type mythifications of the "haptic-audible border" (2018: 91) and its preternatural but often-overestimated powers.
7. With this, Bohlman moves an ethnomusicology of music and religion into considerations of media, markets, identity, and the transformation of sacred repertoires into world music (Bohlman 1997)—ethnomusicological approaches that expanded precipitously in the following decades.
8. See al Faruqi 1985, Nasr 1997, and Shiloah 1995 for ethnomusicological perspectives on music in Islam in this period.
9. For perspectives from Buddhism, see Chen 2001, Greene, et al. 2002, Mabbett 1993, Qing and San 1994, and Wei 1992.
10. This work includes Chernoff 1979, Feld 1982, Seeger 1987, and Shelemay 1989.
11. On Christianity's challenging proximity to anthropology's and ethnomusicology's historical commitments, see Cannell 2005, Engelhardt 2009, and Reily and Dueck 2016.
12. Here, Rouget continues to develop John Blacking's earlier observation that both initiation and "the music itself" matter in trance performance. "And yet the music

does not send any Venda into a trance: it sends only members of the possession cult," Blacking writes, "and then only when they are dancing at their own homes, with which the spirits of the ancestors who possess them are familiar. The effectiveness of the music therefore depends on the context in which it is both performed and heard; but ultimately it depends on the music itself" (1971: 102). Thanks to Martin Stokes for bringing this bit from Blacking's work to my attention.

13. The phenomenon of solitary trance is something that captures Judith Becker's interest in neurobiological and nonsecular approaches to trance, which I take up in Chapter 2.
14. Cf. Racy 1991 on the related concept of *ṭarab* in ecstatic listener/performer feedback loops that decenter musical "works" in ethnomusicology.
15. These include al Faruqi 1985, During 1988, Gribetz 1991, Lewisohn 1997, Nasr 1997, Nelson 1985, Sakata 1983, Sawa 1985, and Shiloah 1995.
16. For an invaluable reassessment of music, listening, the sonic arts, and Islamic legal interpretation in modern Turkey, see Korkmaz and Stokes (2024).
17. For more on the disctinctions between ghinā' and mūsīqā, see al Faruqi 1985: 6; Nelson 1985: 34; Rouget 1985: 256; and Sakata 1983: 40.
18. See Gribetz 1991: 44–45 and Shiloah 1995: 32–33 on these interpretations of Qur'ānic impermissibility.
19. On the permissibility of audition, see Gribetz 1991: 45 and Shiloah 1995: 32.
20. But see Stokes 2002 and Lucas 2012 on the Orientalist trappings of this development.
21. For a reassessment of al Faruqi's thinking on musical legitimacy within Muslim hierarchies, see Garvey 2020.

2
Entangling Religion

Theological terms and concepts carried over from sacred musicologies have a rich, durable presence in ethnomusicology. Theology—words and knowledge of an "inquiry into divine otherness" (Furani 2019: 18)—permeates the language ethnomusicologists think with: *rasa/ras* (the aesthetic expression of unity with an ultimate reality in Indian and Javanese arts); *ṭarab* (the heightened emotionality or ecstasy of performer/listener feedback loops in traditional Arab and Sufi musics); *kavanah* (the spiritual intention and concentration of performing Jewish sound); shout (up-tempo, backbeat-heavy instrumental praise breaks in the Black gospel tradition accompanying spirit-filled dance); *anhad* (the undifferentiated vibration of oneness in Sikh mysticism), and the list could go on. The crossings of the theological and ethnomusicological through these keywords suggest that ethnomusicology may have never been secular (cf. Latour 1993) despite its methodological atheism and agnosticism and the disentangling of music and religion I trace in the previous chapter. Put differently, ethnomusicology, once normatively secular in its disentangling of music and religion, increasingly recognizes the nonsecular in its genealogies, methodologies, and community of ethnomusicologists—the entanglements of *musicandreligion*. In the story of theistic methodologies, the uptake of theological language, and the deepening recognition of other-than-human agency I document in this chapter, relationships with other-than-human agents—relational ontologies and epistemologies—move toward a more fulsome center in ethnomusicology.[1]

As we encountered in Melvin Butler's work in the Introduction, methodological theism is a stance entirely compatible with a critical ethnomusicology. And as we will encounter later in this chapter, the community of ethnomusicologists whose positions and knowledge as religious practitioners inform their work is a significant presence in

Music and Religion. Jeffers Engelhardt, Oxford University Press.
 DOI: 10.1093/9780190699185.003.0003

the discipline. Scholars in this vein who come to mind include Pi-yen Chen (2001, 2010), Steven Friedson (1996, 2009), Hager El Hadidi (2022), Katherine Hagedorn (2001), Cory Hunter (2022), Monique Ingalls (2018), Alisha Lola Jones (2020), Braxton Shelley (2021, 2023), Jeffrey Summit (2000, 2016a), and Tamara Turner (2023). Further still, in addition to enfolding the knowledge of religious practice and positionality, an entangled ethnomusicology uses theological terms and concepts (including sound and vibration per se) reflexively as one way of recognizing the sonic presence of other-than-human agents. Scholars in this vein that come to mind include Andrew Alter (2019), Sarah Bakker Kellogg (2025), Guy Beck (1993), Gurminder Kaur Bhogal (2017, 2023), Sebanti Chatterjee (2023), Rebecca Dirksen (2019), Judit Niran Frigyesi (2018), Richard Jankowsky (2010, 2021), Inderjit Kaur (2016, 2021a, 2021b), Lanlan Kuang (2019), and Richard David Williams (2020).

This chapter follows turns toward an entangled ethnomusicology that mark the increasingly unexceptional presence of theistic methodologies and theologically shaped epistemologies in the field. The ethnomusicology I write about here is positioned, largely implicitly, in proximity to work in anthropology, history, and religious studies concerned with nonsecular ethnography, theologically shaped knowledge, and decolonization. This convergence is not by accident. Rather, it is an alignment of responses to disciplinary crises voiced through resistance to the universalizing, colonizing paradigms of secularity, sovereign human reason, extractive ethnographic enclosure, and whiteness.[2]

Ethnomusicology, Theology, and Taking Seriously

One way of interpreting these resistant responses is to return to the issue of other-than-human agency that has been a through line in this book. In anthropology and ethnographic disciplines, the uptake of actor-network theory, new materialism, new vitalism, object-oriented ontology, models of distributed agency, and perspectivism; critiques of the discipline's secular unconscious; and the recognition of theology as theory have instituted spaces for other-than-humans and what anthropologist Yasmin Moll calls a "Godly ethnography" (2023). And at a less explicit register, the entangled ethnomusicology I write about below follows suit.

We can trace the contours of these responses through a common theme: a dissatisfaction with the ethnographic imperative to take others/difference/ontologies seriously. On the surface, this is a laudable first principle: an opening for ethnography as an exercise in humility and an ethical gesture in the direction of decolonization. Indeed, important work for understanding the range of ways other-than-humans are real is written in just this vein. Anthropologist Tanya Luhrmann's (2012, 2020) writing on the work of the imagination in making God real is a sign of anthropology's broader comfort with recognizing the agency of other-than-human beings—of taking them seriously. Luhrmann's twofold point is that "the invisible other" (but inaudible?) "must be made real for people, and that this real-making changes those who do it" (2020: xii). In a minimally nonsecular frame, other-than-human beings produce change, which is part of their reality as agents. With Lurhmann, God spills over from theology into the ethnographically real.

Others have noted the implications of Luhrmann's twofold approach, beginning with its "break with how the divine is normally portrayed in ethnography—which is normally solely as a warrant for human action, reflexive and otherwise" (Bialecki 2014: 43). As anthropologist Jon Bialecki observes, in a "flat ontology" in which "all objects are equally objects" (itself a challenge to methodological atheism), the "composite object" of an other-than-human being made real through prayer, worship, and ritual effects change at a level exceeding the individual. "As a greater composite object," Bialecki writes, "God displays an effective 'will' autonomous of those who in effect produce Him" (2014: 42). For anthropology, this unsettles the position that "human creations cannot exceed the capacities endowed by their creators" (2014: 34).

For critics, this kind of taking others/difference/ontologies seriously is not enough, since the composite object of a god made real is still both made (placed in scare quotes, perhaps) and an object of coloniality within regnant disciplinary norms. The inherent secularity of this kind of taking seriously insists on "the cultural" within regimes of sovereign reason and the "anthropological atheism" (Ewing 1994) of the discipline.[3] For anthropologist Khaled Furani, ethnographic disciplines are in need of a theological redeeming—"a theistically driven revitalization" (2019: 177)—that might recognize rather than police ultimate difference and otherness—God—beyond the confines of cultural difference (cf. the emergence of disentangled, culturalist ethnomusicology described in Chapter 1). A stubborn coloniality remains, however: "While anthropologists need not deny, nor admit, God's existence," writes Furani, "they must forswear God's relevance to their sovereign reason" (2019: 19). Conventional practices of taking others/difference/ontologies seriously, then, have a limit: as decolonizing projects, they take seriously insofar as they stop short of questioning the secular epistemology of our disciplines. The secular, even as it is critiqued and disavowed, is still "the epistemic unconscious" (Moll 2023: 3) of decolonization, its immanent frame (Taylor 2007).

As the anthropologist Yasmin Moll points out, while taking others/difference/ontologies seriously can "provincialize the ethnographic stance" by transformatively questioning inherited norms and biases, it is nevertheless enfolded in a post-Enlightenment tradition of the sovereign questioning of authority, regardless of one's politics (2023: 10). Taking others/difference/ontologies seriously, in other words, is put in service of critique as a privileged form of human knowing. Provocatively, Moll's Godly ethnography entails something different: positing "God's uniqueness and sovereignty as the one and only creator of the universe" and locating "human variation across time and space within divine unity" (2023: 6).[4] Indeed, as the anthropologist Saba Mahmood (2005) has shown, the secular assumption that critiquing rather than inhabiting authoritative norms is the path to becoming an autonomous subject can itself be critiqued and provincialized (cf. Bakhle 2008: 264). For Moll, "decolonization is a question of restoring the universality of uncorrupted divine self-disclosure—that is, the Qur'an—as the epistemic terrain for analyzing, theorizing, and evaluating human difference across time and space" (2023: 4). Moll's nonsecular, Godly ethnography ends up provincializing the idea of taking others/difference/ontologies seriously in a this-worldly rather than an other-worldly orientation. It can bring ethnography beyond a world of human-centered certainties to include an unknowable, more-than-human beyond.[5]

Opening out, these nonsecular methods echo Joel Robbins's hopes for disciplinary renewal through "engagement with theological ideas that anthropology has previously found alien" (Robbins 2020: 20). By making theological "stranger-concepts" (da Col and Graeber 2011: vii) theoretical and, therefore, potentially universal in the same sense as Western theoretical concepts, theology can push beyond taking others/difference/ontologies seriously toward the entanglements of decolonizing practices. An openness to knowledge of divine otherness—and engagements with theories drawn out of that knowledge—entangles disciplines in productive ways. Robbins (2020: 131–144) offers as an example a rethinking of the classic anthropological category of the gift in light of Christian theologies of passivity: since, in Lutheran theology, one cannot participate as an agent in one's own salvation, the gift of God's grace must be passively received, transforming the Maussian gift-receiver into a patient rather than an agent. More generally, Robbins understands the value of theologically informed theory through its entanglements across disciplinary differences. Theology raises a "God question" for anthropology and ethnomusicology: do spiritual beings have their own agency or, at the end of the day, is that agency an artifact of what humans do in their name (2020: 145)? Lingering at the disciplinary differences this question entails means recognizing methodological theism and nonsecular, entangled positionalities that unsettle the grounds of our practices away from sovereign reason and toward relationship. To this end, Robbins asks: "if God and other spiritual beings exist as agents in the world in more than a socially constructed sense, would there be room for anthropology as we know it?" (2020: 150).

Outlines of an Entangled Ethnomusicology

The same could be said for ethnomusicology, of course: if God and other spiritual beings sing, gift sound, and listen, is there room for a Blackingesque ethnomusicology? The stakes of entangling religion are high when understood in the context of ethnomusicology's dominant secularity, Eurologics, white epistemologies, and decolonizing interventions. As the anthropologist Amira Mittermaier asks in one of this book's epigraphs, "What if, as a Sufi interlocutor of mine in Cairo says, it is about singing to God, not talking about God" (2021: 27)? Would this be recognizable as ethnomusicology, or would we have to call it praise, prayer, worship, or theology?

Jim Sykes's work on musical giving and sonic generosity in Sri Lanka (2018) and critique of music studies' secularity (2020) are notable for taking up many of the central issues in an entangled ethnomusicology. Central to Sykes's project is moving beyond "the music and identity episteme" (2018: 4) that dominates music studies: music (the object, the commodity, the expression of an individual self) produces identities and places. Possible encounters with sound beyond the music and identity episteme include sonic causality (perhaps apart from human agency); sounds as "gifts that *must* be given as gestures of respect to the divine powers, since the gods are by nature not benign but judicial" (2018: 6); the fact that "certain sounds were in the first instance offerings to god(s)" and later subsumed into histories and ethnographies that obscure human–divine relations (2018: 5); and ethnomusicologies of a Buddhist "not-self" (*anatta*). In Sykes's post–civil war Sri Lanka, the entanglements of other-than-human agents in musical giving and ethnomusicological practice trouble the fixity of religion and ethnicity in the music and identity episteme—a crucial part of post-war reconciliation. "The Beravā's [Sinhala Buddhist drummers] musical gifts in the Bera Pōya Hēvisi ['Auspicious Drumming on a Full Moon Night']," Sykes writes,

> are the drum-speech the gods played to celebrate the Buddha's Enlightenment, and they are headed back to the gods. Once we define some music as things that originated with and can (or must) be exchanged with nonhumans, and once we accept sonic efficacy as ontologically valid, certain musical traditions that the identity paradigm construes as belonging only to one ethnic or religious group emerge as having a multi-ethnic or multi-religious history. (2018: 48)

Centering the sonic relationships of humans and other-than-humans in ethnography and historiography restores the status of music as divine offering, protection, or a "sacrifice of praise" (Hebrews 13:15).[6] This move, in turn, creates space for work that troubles the rigid sacred/secular distinctions around which much ethnomusicology has formed, recognizing the entanglements of music and religion in other-than-human agency, theological language, and nonsecular methodologies.

In other work that historicizes and provincializes the secular as a normative musical frame, the historian Janaki Bakhle (2005, 2008) begins from the position that

> it is a matter of routine to witness within the world of music (and dance, and theater) actions and gestures that are not easily categorized as either secular or religious; ritual obeisance to one's teacher or chanting mantras and saying prayers before a performance are examples. (2008: 262)

Tracking how music that is "neither secular nor religious" (2008: 263) is made ostensibly secular in its rescuing for the nation, Bakhle (2005) documents the classicization of Hindustani music through the modernizing reforms of Vishnu Narayan Bhatkhande (1860–1936) and Vishnu Digambar Paluskar (1872–1931). Bhatkhande, a secular musicologist who was trained in law, worked to rationally reclassify Hindustani *rāgas* into a system of ten *ṭhāṭs*, casting off as outdated ancient Sanskrit treatises like the *Natyashastra* that he felt bore little relation to contemporary practices while seeking to harmonize the systems of Hindustani and Carnatic music in service of a unified nation. Despite his "anti-Muslim prejudice, his Brahminic elitism, and his privileging of theory over practice," Bhatkhande's modernist "thirst for proof, demonstrability, documentation, history, and order" (2005: 99) set the terms for a modern *rāga* theory he championed as uncoupled from religion and spirituality, *ustāds* (Muslim master musicians), and *gharānās* (hereditary musical lineages and their disciples) and transmitted, instead, through standardized curricula at state schools. Bakhle stresses, however, that current musical practice "bears little resemblance to Bhatkhande's actual work and writings" (2005: 100).

Paluskar, a populist *bhakti* nationalist, brought a performer's perspective and a more complex form of secularism to the work of modernization. Central to Paluskar's neotraditional project was a revitalization of the *guru–shishya parampara* (teacher–disciple lineage) in service of an ideal of "the natural inextricability of Indian art from Brahminized Hindu sacrality" (2005: 138). This was institutionalized in the state-funded schools Paluskar established, open to women and invested in linking musical performance not with entertainment but with Hindu devotion (bhakti). The secularism of Paluskar's mission brought musical performance out of courts and temples into public, non-religious spaces, but with musicians imagined as spiritual leaders of the nation. This secular gesture, in turn, hardened the public alignments of religion and musicians. Whereas "court and temple musicians in earlier periods had participated in sanctified rituals in both directions, Hindu and Muslim, without that participation interfering with their religious self-definition," Bakhle writes, following Paluskar:

> Muslimness needed to be hidden from view, toned down, or reformulated. It had to *demonstrate* (what it might previously have both accommodated and welcomed) its participation in Brahminic ritual, prayers, *bhajans, kirtans,* and *abhangs* [musical devotions], and attendance at temples as proof of its right to membership in the Indian nation. (2005: 174–175)

This is the crux of Bakhle's "music as the sound of the secular" (2008) not only for secularism debates in India but for ethnomusicology's secular unconscious (cf. Kalra 2015). By thinking and writing within the religious logics of different secularisms, even when pointing to secularism's enchantments (Engelhardt 2015), ethnomusicology does the work of disentangling music and religion, creating boundaries instead of recognizing relationships, circumscribing the agency of other-than-humans, and defaulting to a "modern Western ontology of music" (Sykes 2020: 120). If Sykes's and Bakhle's work helps provincialize a disentangled ethnomusicology, where do we continue our encounter with an entangled ethnomusicology?

Listening Deeply

Let me begin with Judith Becker's landmark study *Deep Listeners: Music, Emotion, and Trancing* (2004). In *Deep Listeners*, Becker critically revisits ethnomusicology's humanistic, ethnographic, and neurobiological approaches to religious trancing (and, by extension, non-religious deep listening). Becker links her work with Sufi qawwals at the Nizamuddin Shrine in New Delhi, Balinese *bebuten* trancing, *bissu* trancing in Sulawesi, and Pentecostal Christians in the United States to her reading of classics from the ethnomusicological literature (Rouget, Qureshi, and others) and her immersion in the neurobiological literature on emotions, perception, and consciousness. In *Deep Listeners*, Becker shows that trancing is at once highly scripted and predictable, intimately connected to music and sound, incompatible with a Cartesian model of the self, gendered and pathologized in Western academic spaces, and, to ethnomusicology's detriment, a field of intellectual fragmentation. One way of reading Becker is to return to the anthropologist Tanya Luhrmann's work on making God real: other-than-human agents must be made real, and that process shapes the people who make those agents real. For Becker, music "enacts" (2004: 27) and "facilitates" this making real through "religious trance (dance, prophecy, speaking in tongues, speaking in voices of spiritual beings)" that shapes the "inner physiology" of those being musicked (2004: 4) and their "dense cultural networks of knowing and feeling" (2004: 38).[7] From this position, Becker's methodological agnosticism in *Deep Listeners* is capacious enough to embrace the entanglement of music and religion—the "special gnosis" (2004: 2) that need not be denied or explained away in a secular humanistic or neurobiological frame.

What positions *Deep Listeners* in a story of entangled ethnomusicology is Becker's idea, expanded from Bourdieu, of a "habitus of listening." A habitus of listening is the conditions of possibility for trancing to happen: musical and sonic cues, scripted ritual roles, social relationships that validate trancing, and atmospheres that cultivate neuronal connections to allow "the trancer to see extraordinary sights, to hear more intensely than one normally would, and to experience emotions that stimulate feelings of closeness to the holy" (2004: 117).

A habitus of listening is supra-individual rather than the world of an autonomous subject; it is formed through the relationship of human and other-than-human agents, irreducible to neurobiology:

> The incipient trancer, through repeated participation in a religious ritual, comes to know the script of the ritual and gradually comes to enact that script herself. As belief is intensified through action, the incipient trancer allows internal physical changes in brain and body that may eventually also allow for trancing. The mind and body of the trancer becomes structurally coupled with the drama of the ritual. Her belief, imagination, sense of self, and *habitus of listening* are coordinated with those of the other human participants and the projected presences of holy beings, the cosmic drama that all enact. (2004: 121–122)

Becker's habitus of listening stands in contrast with the disentangling of music and religion in a key way. The veracity of trancing—the question of "faking" and "trance performance"—has long been made an issue in secular ethnomusicologies by seeking out universal, causal musical characteristics of trance behavior or pointing to the predictability and expedient functionality of trancing. Other-than-human agency, in other words, has not been recognized in many ethnomusicological theorizations of trance. Becker's habitus of listening, however, does something different. Positioned, following Luhrmann, as the sonic/social/spiritual space of "making real," Becker's entangled approach to trancing incorporates the "problem" of genuine trance at the same time it is disinterested in that problem. By extension, this is the problem of religious belief and faith in "kindling the presence" (Luhrmann 2020) of other-than-human beings. Trancers' "fully articulated theories of what is happening" (Becker 2004: 42) are their understandings of how other-than-human agency is real and otherwise-inaccessible knowledge and relationships are accessed. To dwell on the veracity of trancing is to wrench an entangled world of musicked bodies and other-than-human agents into a colonizing habitus of listening emptied of the gods, spirits, and divinities religious practitioners are in relationship with, and this is one extent to which Becker takes other-than-humans seriously.

For Becker, trancers are profoundly in control of themselves; the stereotypicity of trance is trancers' skill at controlling their minds and bodies rather than "a result of fraudulence, of chicanery" (2004: 68). In this way, we can read Becker's writing on Balinese bebuten trancing, apart from the (non-)issue of veracity, as an account of reality rather than a questioning of reality:

> No Balinese music is more demonic, louder, or more minimalist than that which signals the encounter between the witch Rangda and the entranced men who attempt to thwart her power. The driving, incessant ostinatos of these themes are iconic of the emotions of fear and rage and the action of fighting. They undergird and sustain the manic frenzy of both the witch and her attackers. The gamelan music impacts physically on the men who participate; groups of neurons in the brains and bodies of the trancers are firing synchronously with the gamelan rhythms. The clanging bronze keys of the metallophones, the booming gongs, and the pulsing rhythms of drums and cymbals, all synchronized, become one with the body and brain of the trancer. (2004: 142)

Becker's description of the gamelan music accompanying the hostile encounter between Rangda and the enraged bebuten trancers assembles the cultural and the neurobiological into a model of embodied cognition irreducible to either (see Figure 2.1 for her visual representation). As Becker puts it, "fire does not have to be coming from the eyes of the Balinese peasant playing Rangda for the bebuten trancer to see fire coming from her eyes" (2004: 114). The specificity of Becker's ethnographies lead me to make two final points about *Deep Listeners*. First, Becker is resolutely anti-essentialist. Neither trancing nor religion are one thing (2004: 40–43), and attending to a habitus of listening is what situates trancing and religion in history, ensuring against the colonizing deployment of those concepts. Second, Becker anticipates Joel Robbins's call to translate theological concepts as theory. *Rasa*, *tarab*, and *hal* (in Arabic, a condition of ecstasy) are each named in *Deep Listeners* as useful concepts for understanding all forms of trancing, independent of their contexts of origin.

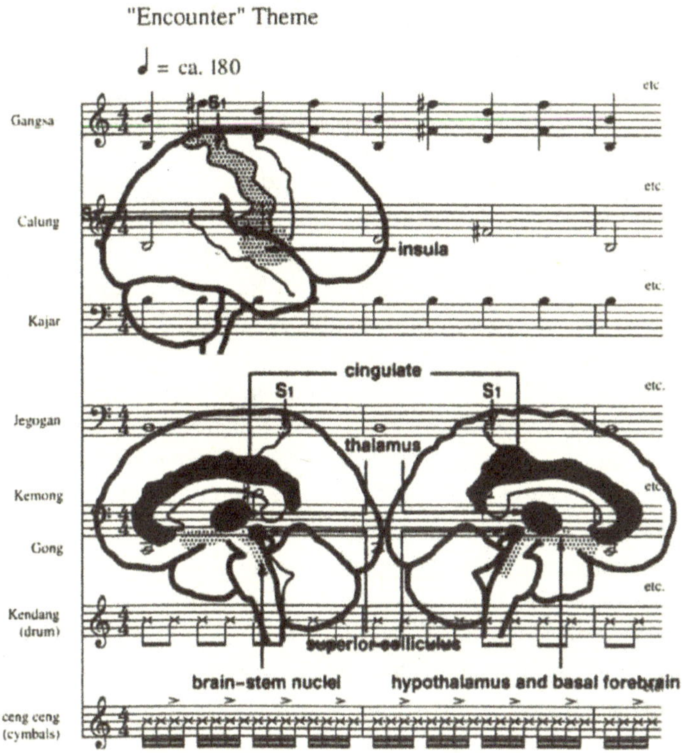

Figure 2.1 Judith Becker's sonic-neurobiological representation (2004: 143) of the encounter between Rangda and her attackers. A trancer's core consciousness is "musicked" by Rangda's gamelan music. (© Judith Becker. Reproduced with permission.)

Theistic Ethnomusicology

If *Deep Listeners* signaled the arrival of an ethnomusicology that recognizes the entanglement of music and religion in other-than-human agency and theological language, it did so from a methodologically agnostic position that, for critics, reproduces the problems of taking others/difference/ontologies seriously. Others work from a methodologically theistic position in which ethnomusicological knowing is entangled with the reality of divinities. In *Divine Utterances: The Performance of Afro-Cuban Santería* (2001), Katherine Hagedorn's theorizing of Santería's (an Afro-Cuban religious tradition of *oricha* worship) sonic theology is intimately linked with her initiation as a priestess of Ochún, her patron oricha. Hagedorn's "making *ocha*" or "making *santo*" became part of her decades-long ethnographic research in Cuba and the United States and position her to know first-hand the "rules of engagement" (2001: 76) at a *toque de santo* (Santería drumming ceremony), the "sacred communicative potential of the *batá* drums, known as *aña*" (2001: 91), the sacred/secular complexities of Santería's "folkloricization" in twentieth-century Cuba, and the gendered and racialized boundaries Santería practitioners enforce in ritual performance.

Hagedorn's ethnomusicology is one that writes against the "ethnocentric reality check" of "belief" (Sahlins 2022: 13) in favor of knowing (rather than merely believing). Through her standing as a daughter of Ochún, oricha of rivers, romantic love, money, and patron saint of Cuba, Hagedorn is able to offer the critical interpretative insight that it is a collectively established "sacred intent" that distinguishes folkloric performances from Santería liturgies. *Batá* drumming on consecrated instruments speaks to the orichas "in their own language" (2001: 100) of "divine utterances" to let them know it is possible to communicate with their human adherents, but this drumming is sonically indistinguishable from folkloric possession performances on unconsecrated instruments staged for tourists and Cuban publics (2001: 111).

The sacred intent that hails the orichas, beckoning them to presence in the body of a "possessed" dancer, is not audible. Indeed, Santería aesthetics are deeply shaped by the professionalism of secular folklore ensembles like the Conjunto Folklórico Nacional de Cuba with whom Hagedorn worked. Here is where Hagedorn's transformation into a nonsecular listener gives her access to the inaudible efficacies of sacred intent at a toque de santo. As she explains, musicians alone cannot bring down an oricha; a collective of invested participants—priests (*Santeros*) and priestesses (*Santeras*) like herself—"sharpens the focus of sacred intent at a *toque*" (2001: 82). At an ethnomusicological moment when the sonic does not produce knowledge of Santería's divine utterances, Hagedorn's nonsecular position offers knowledge of Santería's *aché* (in Yoruba cosmology, a divine power) that is musical (attuned to the channeling of intent through performance) but not sonic. This is a remarkable extension of ethnomusicology beyond the sonic; the theology and ontology of batá drumming as "divinely targeted sound" (Hagedorn 2006) are understood not through a methodologically agnostic approach to its sonic features, for instance, but through the entangled relationships of human intent and oricha presence and action. Coming full circle, the purported secularity of folkloric Santería performance can be infused with sacred intent by nonsecular audiences, cutting across a religious/non-religious boundary that was central to twentieth-century Cuban politics.

One of Hagedorn's key ethnographic moments in *Divine Utterances* comes at a toque honoring Eleguá, trickster and warrior of the crossroads, in Santos Suárez, a suburb of Havana, in 1997. Shortly after the assembled drummers and singers began calling to Eleguá, a young man jumped in front of the drums and "began 'dancing Eleguá'—performing the leaning, off-balance cross steps associated with the mischievous deity, a few to the left, a few to the right, while miming vaudevillian gestures with an imaginary cane (Eleguá's *garabato*, or crooked stick, with which he is said to 'open the road')" (2001: 74). Gradually, the dancer incorporated showy moves from disco and hip-hop, much to the chagrin of the drummers and lead singer. Eventually, Hagedorn's principal teacher Alberto Villarreal stopped playing and sent the young man away, stating "It's an insult—he doesn't have *santo*, and he's not possessed, and he shouldn't be dancing that way. The Santeros and Santeras haven't even danced yet. This is not a disco" (2001: 74).

The young man had violated the "rules of engagement" in a toque, dancing presentationally, not to fulfill the "divine potential of the ceremony" (2001: 76) to bring orichas into presence for blessings, healings, and guidance. At first, Hagedorn was not keyed in to this ritual impropriety, focusing instead on the immediately perceptible poetics of the moment:

> I had been transfixed by his confident manner and radiant movements: the moonwalk, the triple-twirls, the half-splits

> (direct from Michael Jackson's "Thriller" music video). I wondered how they became transformed, translated, and transported to this place of worship, as an offering in front of the sacred *batá* drums for Eleguá, the trickster warrior. Were the dancer's movements deliberate translations from the repertoire of our human trickster, Michael Jackson—who is multiracialized, multigendered, and multitalented—to the arena of the divine trickster Eleguá—who is red on one side and black on the other (to keep his enemies guessing as to his "color"), male and female, and the purveyor of both divine and mundane possibilities? The young dancer's evocation of Michael Jackson for the Mischievous One—with all of its "magic" and skill and newness—seemed a raucous gift, divine in its very profanity. For did he not offer himself up to the musicians (thus to the *orichas*) with a fullness of heart? (2001: 74–75)

As Alberto Villarreal understood, no, the young man did not "have *santo*"; according to the "rules of engagement," and he was judged to be performing an "inappropriate, albeit ingenious, folkloric spectacle" (2001: 83). As Hagedorn's nonsecular positioning took hold in her research, she understood that divinely targeted danced gestures, sung invitations, and drummed sounds were effective for the human/oricha relationships they sustained—a reality not registered in the sonic and the visual, hence the ease of sacred/folkloric confusion. Absent sonic and visual data, one might lean solely into the politics of folkloric Afro-Cuban performance and the financial pressures of catering to tourism in an interpretation of the moonwalking moment, thereby writing out the other-than-human agency a theistic methodology recognizes. "The 'harm,' then, in dancing the moonwalk in front of drums intended for Eleguá," Hagedorn concludes,

> was that Eleguá did not "choose" this man as a dancer; that is, he did not possess him or "make" him do the moonwalk. If the ranking priests and priestesses of Santería and the ritual musicians had been convinced that the young dancer had been possessed, then Michael Jackson's moonwalk would not have been a problem. Rather, it might have become incorporated into other *oricha* possession dances. (2001: 83)

Eventually, Eleguá did arrive at the toque, and Hagedorn uses that moment to connect ritual failure to ritual efficacy, with Eleguá redressing the young man's improprieties as part of his own deviousness and unpredictability. Hagedorn's signal contribution in *Divine Utterances* to the story of an entangled ethnomusicology is how her analyses become final. As a Santería initiate, her epistemological position and scholarly goals lead her to rest her case, so to speak, in the agency of orichas like Eleguá; in their action and (potential or past) presence as an initiating cause. Hagedorn is comfortable that orichas' presence in her work is sufficient to make that work ethnomusicological; she is not required to punt their agency into the "real" of human action and conventional ethnomusicological paradigms. Orichas' presence and Hagedorn's position as a daughter of Ochún ground her analyses of sacred intent in *Divine Utterances*. Rather than divining sacred intent, Hagedorn can know and communicate it in her nonsecular ethnomusicology.

A Black Gospel Episteme

Hagedorn's nonsecular ethnomusicology, informed by knowledge of her relationship with other-than-human agents, continues into the present. As I mention in the Introduction, a coalescing of work in the Black gospel tradition is, in the 2020s, one of the most readily encountered of nonsecular ethnomusicologies. What we might call a Black gospel episteme again begs the question of ethnomusicology having ever been secular, and what kind of gatekeeping practice ethnomusicology's secularity has been. Indeed, an axiom of Black gospel scholarship is the superficiality of distinctions between the sacred and secular, particularly in light of West African and African American ontologies of divine sonic ubiquity.[8] Here, I turn to the entanglements of theology, human/divine relationship, theistic methodologies, and religious leadership in Alisha Lola Jones's *Flaming: The Peculiar Theopolitics of Fire and Desire in Black Male Gospel Performance* (2020) and Braxton Shelley's *Healing for the Soul: Richard Smallwood, the Vamp, and the Gospel Imagination* (2021) to continue expanding ethnomusicology's nonsecular address.

In *Flaming?*, Jones takes on the fraught work of interpreting Black men's aural/visual expressions of gender and sexuality in Pentecostal Christianity and gospel performance. I say fraught because "to transgress conventional gender expression and heterosexual presentation is a theological and political act in Pentecostalism" (2020: 9), and Jones, positioned as an African American, heterosexual woman, Pentecostal minister and musician, and ethnomusicologist, is transgressive in amplifying and critiquing those phenomena (2020: 23). Throughout *Flaming?*, Jones confronts the mistrust and judgment of her interlocutors and the heteropatriarchal structures of the religious institutions she inhabits (2020: 252, n60) in order to write about "what Christian hospitality might sound like" (2020: 224) and "how we interpret the move of the Spirit" (2020: 2) in nonsecular ethnomusicological listening.

At the center of her book is a complicated Pentecostal sonic/worship/moral calculus. Churchgoers rely on the Spirit-anointed bodies and voices of same-gender-loving men or men with queer potential to bring them musically into "meaningful" worship (2020: 25). At the same time, their sexuality is condemned in congregations and from pulpits "despite evidence that these musicians are used by God to convert souls and change lives" (2020: 9). Jones has a penchant for using words' multiple meanings to her critical advantage in interpreting this calculus. In Pentecostal worlds, "peculiar" can refer to those who are spiritually "set apart," "sanctified," or "consecrated" for God's purposes (including Jones herself); it can also refer to "sonic and visual cues, including vocal style, gesture, attire, and homiletics" that position men as transgressive in their gender expression and sexuality (2020: 9). The meanings of "flaming" are fourfold: (1) a deprecatory term for feminine masculinity and queer potential; (2) moments when the presence of the Holy Spirit is real and spiritual fire/bodily desires erupt in speaking in tongues and demonstrative worship—"'fire shut up in my bones'—an adaptation of Jeremiah 20:9" (2020: 9); (3) imagery connected to divine purification, refinement, and judgment; and (4) "a site of queer power reversal" where condemnations of homosexuality "go up in flames" in the face of musical worship leaders' abilities to bring churchgoers to God (2020: 9). Together, peculiarity and flaming are through lines in Jones's work that bind the divine potential of those anointed to lead to the queer potential and unspoken truth of their identities.

Jones's knowledge of the Holy Spirit, Pentecostalism's heteropatriarchy, gospel music's ministering power, and the gendering of vocal sound enable her to listen to peculiarity and flaming in their sonic and theopolitical richness. Put otherwise, a secular listening apart from knowledge of and relationship with Pentecostalism's other-than-human agents would amount to a different kind of ethnomusicology—perhaps one that harms as it reduces peculiar musicians' multivalent abilities to enflame. This is especially important when inhabiting ethnomusicological spaces one finds morally troubling or harmful—Black men's vocal testimonies of "deliverance" from homosexuality, in Jones's case. At the same time, Jones's analysis in the "I am Delivert!" chapter of *Flaming?* is a powerful example of an entangled ethnomusicology's potentials.

"The outcomes of ['deliverance'] rituals," Jones writes, "are conspicuously commemorated in recordings by black male gospel vocalists in which they demonstrate evidence of God's approval; that is, speaking in tongues, changing lives, and facilitating communal encounters with God" (2020: 40). These theopolitical artifacts are meant to ensure that high male singers, sonically stereotyped as feminized and queered (2020: 43), can navigate the surveillance of their gender presentation, sexuality, and music ministry. Jones offers us the example of Pastor Daryl Lynn Coley's "He Delivered Me" from his 1993 album *He's Right on Time: Live in Los Angeles*:

> Coley attests, "He raised me, He saved me, He bought me, He taught me, He filled me, He thrilled me, He kept me . . . " Among the litany of ways in which God delivered him, Coley signifies on vocalized evidence by rolling the "r" (a.k.a. an alveolar voiced or pitched trill) in the word "thrilled," and thus, illustrating the resulting lingual animation of his deliverance—so powerful that it unties the tongue of a man who was once homosexual.
>
> According to Pentecostal belief, one who is in need of deliverance could not possibly provide evidence that the Spirit of God indwells them. One's demonstration of infilling of the Holy Spirit is a criteria for authenticating one's spiritual vitality for setting

> the atmosphere in worship, as opposed to quenching the Spirit due to a lack of spiritual fervor. Thus, "thrilled" becomes a sonic multireferent for spiritual fire, vocal resonance, transformation, pleasure, the exoticism of Latin linguistics, and physical ability by demonstrating the dexterity of his articulators in a manner resembling speaking in tongues: the essential evidence that one is filled with the Holy Spirit in the Pentecostal tradition; thereby, verifying that they are transformed or are no longer "playin' church". (2020: 42–43)

In bringing us to the "phonosonic nexus" (Harkness 2014) of Coley's performance, Jones initially locates his vocal testimony in a version of compulsory Pentecostal heterosexuality. But listening to peculiarity and flaming opens other interpretive spaces—namely, the possibility of understanding Coley's deliverance not from homosexuality but from the condemnation of his churchgoing audiences. Jones continues:

> Tapping into Pentecostal vernacular, queer listeners hear and see the soloist in the song as being liberated from the self-loathing that deliverance rituals and homoantagonistic rhetorics are said to cultivate so much so that he speaks in tongues—and thus provides evidence that he has the Holy Ghost through sexual healing. (2020: 43)

This queer listening inverts the theopolitics of Black men's gospel performance to convey Jones's knowledge of an otherwise Pentecostal sonic/worship/moral calculus. Jones positions herself apart from conservative gender and sexual ideologies where her "perspectives theologically diverge from the community that called me into ministry" (2020: 25). These theopolitical frictions clearly shape Jones's ethnomusicology, and the point to make here is that the theological and the ethnomusicological are productively entangled in Jones's work. Indeed, a theistic methodology that encounters the real agency of the Holy Spirit as ethnographic evidence is especially useful here since it might aid Jones in managing the theopolitical frictions her work engenders. A final methodological note is that Jones's generous practice of citing scripture (see the Jeremiah 20:9 example above) as ethnographic and theoretical text has the effect of overcoming the sacred/secular binary Black music studies have long written against.

Braxton Shelley's *Healing for the Soul* is another slice of the Black gospel episteme—an invitation into the (auto)ethnographic analytical listening of an ordained minister, gospel musician, and music scholar. While nominally focused on gospel legend Richard Smallwood, Shelley's project is trained on something more expansive as well: articulating how voice, language, musical materials and processes, Black Christianity's rhetorical and "choreosonic" (Crawley 2016) traditions, and gospel's "sonifying the divine's appearance in the material world" (Shelley 2021: 35) inform the "Gospel Imagination." Shelley writes about and within the Gospel Imagination, a religious and epistemological space he likens to Becker's "habitus of listening" (2004), and he does so from an explicitly theistic methodological position. *Healing for the Soul* is, among other things, a "musical theology" (2021: 31) that communicates (auto)ethnographic knowledge of how "gospel song alchemizes the materiality of sound into the substance of faith" (2021: 7) and "holds two worlds together" (2021: 39)—a this-world of human frailty and an otherworld of divine, healing power. By attending to Smallwood and other gospel artists in their musical and religious fullness, Shelley reaches for "what seems most important in gospel music: the idea that Jesus's life marked an intrusion of divine power in the material world—an incursion that transformed the course of human history by remaking the relationship between time and eternity" (2021: 105).

To play with one of Shelley's favorite turns of phrase, what does this nonsecular ethnomusicology sound like? We might begin at the Mt. Level Missionary Baptist Church in Durham, North Carolina, where Sister Lawson once exclaimed to Shelley, "I love it when you play that Holy Ghost chord!" (2021: 34). This moment was transformative for Shelley, and it informs his approach to the once-secular analytical metalanguages he transforms in *Healing for the Soul.* Although we never learn its identity, the Holy Ghost chord is an instance of other-than-human presence in musical materials, a presence that is not merely representational (2021: 136), but immanent and available to the bodies and spirits of worshippers and listeners. In the Gospel Imagination, the materials (Roman numeral-identified chords and melodic hooks), temporalities (groove, repetition, and tonal syntax), and forms (call-and-response and anaphora) of conventional music analysis are recast in theological terms, once again reminding us of Joel Robbins's hopes for a discipline's renewal in adopting theology as theory. Shelley's theological terms of analysis, drawn from the vocabulary of gospel artists, music ministers, Black preachers and theologians, and worshippers like Sister Lawson, are many, inhabiting the "interworld" of "being-in-the-spirit, which means an enfleshed presence in two worlds at the same time" (2021: 141). These terms include:

- Tuning up: the heightening of rhetoric at the end of a sermon and the intensification of sound in gospel to move between "Black Christians and the invisible subjects of their belief" (2021: 57).
- Vamp: gospel's "main event" fusing music and movement in an ecstatic "troping cycle" (Ramsey 2003) that transform lyrics into "the living word of God" (Shelley 2021: 19).
- Shout: gospel's "choreosonic fusion of music and dance" (2021: 138) around a characteristic circular, chromatic bassline and strong backbeats that is an "incarnation of joy" (2021: 129).
- *Kairos*: "the consequential moment when multiple, incommensurate forms of temporality achieve a meaningful consonance" (2021: 126) through tuning up; an irruption of eternity ushered in by gospel vamps.
- Incarnation: after Jesus, "the word being made flesh in the bodies of believers" (2021: 193) through the "thing-power" of words and gospel's sacramental capacity to "stand in for the holy" (2021: 194).

Put schematically, Shelley's (auto)ethnographic analysis of the Gospel Imagination connects tuning up (the sermonic transition from speech to song and the transition into a vamp or shout in a gospel song) to the irruption of kairos (eternity in history). Gospel's choreosonics (the entanglements of movement and sound in holy dancing and shouting music) are its incarnational theology: "the more deeply one goes into the body," Shelley writes, "the further one goes into the spirit" (2021: 140).

Smallwood's "Healing" is the title track of Shelley's book and one of his primary examples of the Gospel Imagination as an analytic frame. Guiding readers through a video of "Healing" at a 1998 live performance in Detroit,[9] Shelley's analysis progresses from the poetics of Smallwood's play with harmonic syntax and sermonic rhetoric into the "preacherly" moves Smallwood makes in the vamp and coda of "Healing." Shelley himself "tunes up" in his writing, transitioning from a more conventional harmonic analysis showing how "tonal motion paves the way for the healing musical experience that this song seeks to provide" (2021: 41–42) into a theologically informed interpretation of the song's temporality and sermonic function:

> Smallwood's scream and the new form of his chanted ad libs join the recursive harmonic processes to produce gospel's characteristic moment of inflection, the shift into the vamp, effecting within the song what is often achieved in gospel sermons through the transition from speech into song—tuning up. (2021: 51)

After shifting into the vamp with an ecstatic falsetto scream, Smallwood interpolates the text of Isaiah 53:3 over the song's hook ("There is a balm in Gilead!," a paraphrase of Jeremiah 8:22 evoking the beloved spiritual) sung by Vision, Smallwood's choir. Shelley's transcription is reproduced in Figure 2.2.

(Listen, he was wounded for our transgressions. The word of God say. Hallelujah!)

There is a balm in Gilead!

(And it also says that he was bruised for our iniquity.)

There is a balm in Gilead!

(The chastisement of our peace was upon him.)

There is a balm in Gilead!

(And with his stripes I'm healed! I'm healed! Right now I'm healed!)

Figure 2.2 Braxton Shelley's transcription (2021: 48) of Smallwood's interpolation of Isaiah 53:3 over the hook of "Healing."

The vamp's intensifying recursion and Smallwood's preacherly vocal delivery in "Healing" accomplish what Shelley hears throughout the gospel tradition—an "intercalation" of prophetic pasts and otherwise futures in the present of a song: kairos. For Shelley, the material potential of healing resin from trees in eighth century BCE Palestine is braided with Smallwood's testimony about Isaiah's prophetic message in the vamp. "In this instance, at the song's live recording," Shelley writes,

> as the choir repeatedly sang that "there is a balm in Gilead" the song accrued a performative, sacramental power that transformed their temporal setting into a transcendent space where the balm from Gilead became palpable in their midst. The balm from Gilead became available in Detroit. Thus, Smallwood could repeatedly declare, "It's here!" (2021: 53)

In *Healing for the Soul,* Shelley's nonsecular listening and ministerial stance allow him to recognize the metalanguages of music analysis in theological terms. His (auto)ethnographic field of the Gospel Imagination is a space of incarnational musicking and the movement of other-than-human agents. Together with Alisha Lola Jones, Melvin Butler, and a host of ethnomusicological elders and emerging scholars, Shelley's work announces the arrival of a coherent body of nonsecular ethnomusicology centered around a Black gospel episteme. Their ethnomusicology models not only what centering methodological theism and the knowledge of other-than-human relationships can mean but also how the resurgence of an entangled ethnomusicology can produce a more fulsome center in the field.

Entangling as Ethnomusicological Renewal

The entanglements of *musicandreligion* in twenty-first-century ethnomusicology are part of a disciplinary renewal offering pathways beyond the Eurological, colonizing forces of secularity, extractive enclosure, and sovereign authorship. The ethnomusicology in this chapter draws deeply on the methodological and theoretical developments of new materialism and the nonhuman turn, calls to recognize and translate theology as theory, and scholars' knowledge of and relationships with other-than-human agents. Indeed, an entangled ethnomusicology, whether methodologically agnostic in the style of Becker or methodologically theistic in the style of Hagedorn and the Black gospel episteme, elaborates with particular clarity how sounds' material effects, sacred ontologies, and webs of relationships between human and other-than-human beings matter in the work of renewal. If Luhrmann's "making real" is both a methodology and an epistemology that resonates across disciplines, then ethnomusicology can participate in two complementary ways: through making other-than-human agents real in agnostic/theistic musical ethnographies and through making knowledge of other-than-human agents real in theistic work.

The examples I engage above are not the only moments of entangled ethnomusicology. To close this chapter, I call attention to other work that draws a more complete picture of ethnomusicology encountering religion not only as culturalist difference, but as a problematic, problematizing space for disciplinary renewal. Steven M. Friedson's two books on Tumbuka healing in northern Malawi and Brekete shrines in coastal Ghana bring us into ritual worlds of sacrifice, healing, trance, and what Friedson hears as drumming's "acoustic illusions" interlacing with Christian and Muslim religious practices. In *Dancing Prophets: Musical Experience in Tumbuka Healing* (1996), Friedson's theistic methodology and personal experience of disease and healing brings him into an ethnomusicology of possibility rather than actuality—"participation and openness, not manipulation and control" (1996: xvi). His time spent with Lußemba, a female *nchimi* (prophet) healer, and Saza, his principal *vimbuza* (music and dance used to treat spirit illnesses) drumming teacher, brought him into a world of vimbuza drumming/motional modes whose multidimensional processes create "a sacred clinical reality" (1996: 143) for diagnosing and treating patients. In seeking out what is possible rather than what is, Friedson followed Tumbuka patients into their reported experiences, dancing himself along the boundaries of vimbuza spirit possession where "I could no longer tell whether the drumming was coming from outside or inside my head" (1996: 161).

In *Remains of Ritual: Northern Gods in a Southern Land* (2009), Friedson writes of an "ontomusicology that engages music *as* ritual and ritual *as* music" (2009: 12), refusing to disentangle the two. The Brekete pantheon of northern gods taking root in southern Ewe communities sustains the drumming, clapping, singing, and dancing of shrine ritual—"a soundscape beyond the acoustical, bringing into the world a way of being-there for the gods that is fundamentally a being-away" (2009: 8–9). Being-there for vimbuza spirits means being-away in trance, and Friedson's reframing of the "African hemiola" helps him communicate "the possibility of being-there-and-away" (2009: 140) in ritual participation. The "even odds" of Ewe polymeters are a crossroads (a place for Legba, the Brekete god of crossroads) of two- and three-feels where movement and possibility reside fluidly in vimbuza ritual.

Richard C. Jankowsky continues Friedson's ethnomusicology of possibility in two books on *sṭambēlī* and Sufism in Tunis, Tunisia, that bring readers into the densities and intensities of history, healing, and ritual communities. In *Sṭambēlī: Music, Trance, and Alterity in Tunisia* (2010), Jankowsky translates "ritual's own theoretical potential" (2010: 6) into an interpretation of his experience performing in sṭambēlī rituals, the sub-Saharan sonic geographies and historical imaginaries of his Tunisian coparticipants, the agency of sṭambēlī saints made present through their individual melody (*nūba*), and the healing efficacies of possession trance. In *Ambient Sufism: Ritual Niches and the Social Work of Musical Form* (2021), Jankowsky turns to the "sonic potencies" of ambient Sufism in Tunis—"signifying aesthetic forces that act upon subjects" (2021: 12) to grant rather than wield power. His analytic attention to timbre, texture, musical intensification, and composite musical forms shows how musical form is not a disentangled epiphenomenon but the sonic granting of power that makes ritual efficacious.

Other ethnomusicologists offer us theologically informed theorizing on music's inaudible powers whose uptake in the field exceeds its contexts of origin. In *"Mek Some Noise": Gospel Music and the Ethics of Style in Trinidad* (2007), Timothy Rommen articulates an "ethics of style" in Full Gospel Trinidad that actualizes belief and convinces churchgoers how to "live as and sound like Christians in Trinidad" (2007: 1). Rommen's ethics of style is how Full Gospel Christians negotiate ethical relationships with one another and ethical alterity with other Trinidadians through musical style. In choosing to embrace or disavow styles like North American gospel or Gospelypso in their congregations, Full Gospel Christians enact a theologically informed ethics in which aesthetics (music's audibility) are secondary. "It would be nice if this or that sounds good," Rommen writes, "but if it *is* good then that characteristic will override aesthetic concerns" (2007: 37). Rommen's accomplishment in *"Mek Some Noise"* is to elaborate ethnographically exactly what, for Full Gospel Trinidadians, the "*is* good" amounts to, prior to its sounding.

In a similar vein, Inderjit N. Kaur's "Theorizing the (Un)Sounded in Sikhī: Anhad, Sabad, and Kīrtan" (2021a) is a theologically informed theorization and ethnography of Sikh practices whose terms of analysis can extend beyond Sikh contexts. Kaur meditates here on the term *anhad* (literally, limitless), a sonically rich metaphor found in the Guru Granth Sahib, describing it as "unheard sound" and a "metaphor for ethical potential" (2021a: 2). Kaur's intervention is, with reference to Sikh scriptural verses, to position anhad as an immediate, unproduced, and undifferentiated vibration "common to each entity in the universe" (2021a: 3) and, as such, an experienced attribute of the divine, of "non-Othering" (2021a: 12). Kaur's nonsecular listening to anhad, along with those in her ethnography, brings us to how "Sikhs imbibe Sikhī [teachings]" (2021a: 1) and model a potentially translatable methodology for encountering other relational ontologies of (un) sound.

Finally, in a nonsecular collaborative mode, Byron Dueck and Essele Essele Kisito's "Authority, Deference, and Disregard in Catholic Liturgical Music in Central Cameroon" (2022), presents us with an ethnography of Catholic music in indigenous idioms activating relationships among musicians, ethnographers, and "other-than-human beings" (2022: 22). Together, Dueck, an "agnostic" white Canadian ethnomusicologist, and Essele, a Black Cameroonian ethnomusicologist and Catholic priest, articulate the "relations of deference and obligation" (2022: 44) shaped through contemporary Cameroonian Catholic music. Their complementary relationship as ethnographers yields a non-reductive account of religious obedience and social authority in the cultivation of a doctrinally sound aesthetics at the Catholic University of Central Africa in Yaoundé.

The entangled ethnomusicology I think with in this chapter is nonsecular in two complementary senses. First, it recognizes the theological as another form of theory that might offer critical interpretive purchase in other ethnomusicological spaces. In the process, it recognizes with increasing confidence and subtlety the other-than-human agents that are disentangled and written out of secular, culturalist ethnomusicology. Second, in its theistic forms, the entangled ethnomusicology in this chapter closes the gaps between knowledge of religion and knowledge through religion. Ethnomusicologists' relationships with Robert Orsi's "special beings" (2016) and what Marshall Sahlins calls "metapersons" (2022) constitute their epistemological positions and need not be bracketed off in the name of sovereign reason or disciplinary gatekeeping.

In their ambitious forms, entangled, antiracist, decolonizing ethnomusicologies push beyond taking others/difference/ontologies seriously within the discipline's secular unconscious and toward transformation—transformation that might make English-dominant, Eurological ethnomusicology feel more like its sacred musicological precursors and neighboring traditions of music studies that have long incorporated the theological. As Amira Mittermaier (2021) reminds us, the other-than-human can also be the more-than-human, circumscribing the humble limits of what ethnomusicologists can know and creating positive spaces for unknowability and meaninglessness in the discipline.[10] A question hovers over this late moment in the book, then: is entangled encounter with its promise of renewal and fulsomeness the only viable ethnomusicology of music and religion?

Notes

1. Ethnomusicology's other-than-human agents are, just like their human counterparts, thoroughly historical and always emergent—what Robert Orsi calls an "abundant history" set against "modernity's ontological singular" (2016: 59).
2. One only needs to tune into the work of The Society for Ethnomusicology's Crossroads Section for Difference and Representation or read the disciplinary critiques of Stephen Amico (2020), John Garzoli and Tharanat Hin-on (2023), Virinder S. Kalra (2015), Jessica Bissett Perea and Gabriel Solis (2019), and Dylan Robinson (2020) to understand the stakes and extent of ethnomusicology's crises.

3. For more on the sense of inadequacy in taking others/difference/ontologies seriously, see the conversations on "challenging anthropology's rootedness in the ontology of the Enlightenment, or secularism" (2) in light of theology in Meneses and Bronkema (2017).
4. Moll's Godly ethnography is oriented toward the "pluriversity" (Mbembe 2016) of epistemic and methodological decolonization. From her Muslim perspective, "Islamic anthropology predicates not a sovereign human subject but a sovereign God" (2023: 4). This contrasts, in my reading, with the ethnomusicologically adjacent field of ethnodoxology, whose goals include "nurturing local expressions of [Christian] worship" (Swijghuisen Reigersberg and Schrag forthcoming: 1) through missionization and inculturation—often framed in the language of taking difference seriously. See Muriel Swijghuisen Reigersberg and Brian Schrag's chapter on ethnodoxology (forthcoming) for a full assessment.
5. Anthropologist Amira Mittermaier (2021), in a meditation on the phrase *Allāhu akbar* (God is greater), prefers the term "more-than-humans" to "other-than-human" while acknowledging that minimizing the position of the human comes from a place of security and privilege. Throughout, I use "other-than-human" rather than the negatively framed "nonhuman" as an inclusive way of writing about gods, spirits, deities, demons, and agentive things.
6. For more on music and sound as divine offerings and sources of protection in Theravada Buddhist traditions in Sri Lanka and Myanmar, see, respectively, Deegalle (2022) and Douglas (2020).
7. Julia Cassaniti and Tanya Luhrmann write of this as the "cultural kindling" of phenomenological experiences of divine presence or spiritual movement, suggesting that "the local culture of a particular religion" shapes "the way people pay attention to what they sense and feel in search of evidence of the spiritual" and lowers "the threshold of its identification through the body" (2014: S341). The implication here is that different religions "kindle" different experiences of other-than-human presence and agency.
8. Here I am thinking of a strand in the long tradition of Black music scholarship informing the work I engage in this section, including Boyer (1979), Burnim (1983, 1985), Djedje (1978), Keyes (2009), Maultsby (1983, 1992), Ramsey (2003), Reed (2003, 2012), and Southern (1977, 1997).
9. Video of this performance is available on the book's website: https://global.oup.com/us/companion.websites/9780197566466/res/ch1/1/
10. For more on the positive value of meaninglessness, see Gerety (2016).

Conclusion

Religion's Inaudibility

My short answer to that question is no. Entangled, nonsecular ethnomusicology is not the only viable way to encounter music and religion. To claim otherwise would chafe against ethnomusicology's ongoing decolonization by imposing a universal epistemology and methodology on the field. What *Music and Religion* shows is that ethnomusicology has gone around its nonsecular turn for good, meaning that culturalist, human-centered ethnomusicologies that disentangle intermingle productively (in journals, on bookshelves, and in collaborations across difference) with ethnomusicologies that entangle human and other-than-human beings in relationships of knowing and sacred sonic exchange. Such intermingling is what led me to group together the three epigraphs that open this book. Zora Neale Hurston's questioning probes the how, who, and where of the sacred's making in language potentially open to secular and nonsecular responses. Judith Becker's questioning probes the possibilities and pitfalls of a belief-based approach to sonic religious experience, also inviting potentially secular and nonsecular responses.[1] And Amira Mittermaier's questioning probes the limits of secular knowledge and the potential for knowledge in nonsecular, human/other-than-human sonic relationships, inviting us to revisit the grounds of our scholarly enterprises.

Two recent examples can make this intermingling tangible. In *Singing a Hindu Nation: Marathi Devotional Performance and Nationalism* (2013), Anna Schultz refutes the modern, secular notion that religion and politics are, ideally, separate spheres, meaning that religion is something to be (de)politicized. Schultz traces the anticolonial emergence, reforms, and contemporary Hindutva-aligned practice of *rāṣṭrīya kīrtan* (nationalist, bhakti devotional performance) through

Music and Religion. Jeffers Engelhardt, Oxford University Press.
 DOI: 10.1093/9780190699185.003.0004

the frame of "devotionalizing nationalism"—salvation through the sacred storytelling of a Hindu nation.[2] In *Singing a Hindu Nation*, we encounter the currency of disentangling music and religion in order to critique their very separation.

In *Efficacy of Sound: Power, Potency, and Promise in the Translocal Ritual Music of Cuban Ifá-Òrìṣà* (2023), Ruthie Meadows attends to sonic possibility in Ifá divination and "the transformative potential of the òrìṣà to aid in solving real-world problems within conditions of human precarity" (2023: 5). The efficacious sounds of Ifá-Òrìṣà "resolve" and help Cuban practitioners "get by" materially and spiritually in life, and this is the entanglement that Meadows recognizes in *Efficacy of Sound*. Sound in Nigerian-style Ifá-Òrìṣà is a "means of heightened communication between humans and Ifá/òrìṣà" (2023: 14) that grounds knowledge of ritual potential in Cuban social ecologies.

My wordplay with *musicandreligion* throughout this book ultimately signifies a disciplinary moment in which music and religion are at once reified, commonplace secular categories at work in the world and an assemblage that exceeds the histories and limits of those categories.[3] My fuller answer to the question that ends Chapter 2 aims to push past ethnomusicology's habit of asking "what music adds" (Stokes 2023: 7) to prior, higher-value knowledge established elsewhere (in anthropology, religious studies, and history, in this case). After sharing another vignette like the one from the Mt. Calvary Holy Church Christian Restoration Centre in Nairobi I opened with to ground a (dis)entangled ethnomusicological praxis, I will linger over what ethnomusicology's non-derivative interventions in the study of music and religion can be.

Can You Feel It?

In 2005, sacred steel gospel artists The Campbell Brothers visited my home institution of Amherst College for the first time for a performance and conversation. The Campbell Brothers (seen in Figure C.1) are widely celebrated bearers of the sacred steel gospel music tradition nurtured since the 1930s in the House of God (Keith Dominion) and the Church of the Living God (Jewell Dominion) churches—African American Holiness-Pentecostal denominations found across the United States. Sacred steel gospel gets its sound and name from the foregrounded presence of pedal and lap steel guitar in the style, introduced into the Keith Dominion by brothers Troman, Willie, and Henry Eason in the late 1930s/early 1940s and the Jewell Dominion by Lorenzo Harrison in the early 1940s. Steel guitars' presence in the Keith and Jewell Dominions was part of the "Hawaiian guitar" (*kikā kila*) vogue emerging from Joseph Kekuku's *kī hōʻalu* or slack-key style that transformed popular music in the United States in the early decades of the twentieth century.[4] In the following decades, Henry Nelson, Robert Randolph, Glenn Lee, Sonny Treadway, Aubrey Ghent, and The Campbell Brothers brought sacred steel closer to the gospel mainstream and, to varying degrees, into spaces beyond House of God and Church of the Living God worship.

At their performance in Amherst, The Campbell Brothers—Chuck, Darick, Carlton, and Phil Campbell—played material from their 2005 Ropeadope release *Can You Feel It?* and gospel classics, but not the praise, shout, and jamming music of Holiness-Pentecostal worship that creates atmospheres for listeners to fall out in Holy Spirit-infused dance and glossolalia. The powers of sacred steel are many: the kinetic

Figure C.1 The Campbell Brothers—Chuck, Darick, Carlton, and Phil, clockwise from upper left. (© Jim Brock. Reproduced with permission.)

effects of up-tempo backbeat "framming," the at-ease shuffle of a mid-tempo gospel hymn, or unexpected harmonic moves around a beloved melody. But it is the steel guitar's capacity to speak, sing, growl, sweeten, quake, and run melodically; to weave around a rhythmic groove, flash across the fretboard, and tarry around pitches; and to dominate in volume, tone, and sound a church or performance venue in the hands of a master artist like the late Darick Campbell that defines the world of sacred steel.

With exacting knob and pedal control over the envelope and tonal qualities of their sound and the liquid slide of pitches under the steel bar, sacred steel guitarists can sing as song surrogates in familiar hymns and gospel treatments—Darick Campbell's rendering of Sam Cooke's "A Change Is Gonna Come" spoke in this non-metaphorical sense to the Amherst audience.[5] Sacred steel's proximity to the human voice centers it in House of God and Church of the Living God prayer and meditation by channeling a player's testimony, understanding of, and material contact with the word like a gospel singer's. Famously, singers would stop singing to hear Henry Nelson speak through a sacred steel gospel hymn. Their tonal turns, articulations, and breathing network instrument, body, and familiar lyrics in an amplified, extended voice.[6] At other moments, sacred steel guitarists translate ecstatic gestures of praise and shout to their instrument through electrifying vibrato, growling sonorities, feverish accelerations of tempo and intensifying harmonic textures, and acrobatic leaps that both sonify and guide the holy dancing at the front of a church or, in Amherst, the movement of bodies in a club space during the breakdown of a gospel blues number.

The sonic-spiritual power of sacred steel gospel moves from word to body and from Holiness-Pentecostal worship to nonchurch performance venues and back again, tracing Braxton Shelley's (2021) interworldly paths between the spiritual and the material and movement between postures of listening that may or may not involve relationships with other-than-human agents. Moving alongside one another, entrained by sacred steel's driving grooves, mentally taking up the words the guitar speaks, the bodies present at a Campbell Brothers performance foreground the (dis)entanglements of music and religion not only for ethnomusicologists but also for churchgoing musicians and listeners, nonreligious audiences, and those positioned otherwise.

The Campbell Brothers spoke to this in conversation at Amherst, rearticulating histories of play between Saturday night and Sunday morning in Black music and the Black church, others' misgivings about gospel musicians performing in nonchurch venues for the unsaved or the appetites of white listeners, and the personal and spiritual challenges they face because of their careers. Chuck Campbell, pedal steel player in The Campbell Brothers and, along with his brothers, raised in the family of Bishop Charles Campbell, described the dynamic of nonchurch performances: embodied responses to their music are outwardly similar in church and nonchurch atmospheres—hypothetically, a Holiness-Pentecostal believer and an unsaved fan could be dancing and moving the same way, side by side, expressing sonic experiences indexing spiritual movement and/or performers' mastery. The ambiguity of these scripted, predictable movements in the affective atmospheres of church and nonchurch performance (Is the shout authentic? Is that a fan or a believer?) is an everyday part of Chuck Campbell's musicking and religious life, and reconciling the Holy Spirit's movement and his own musical charisma in nonchurch sacred steel performance was something Campbell was happy to leave undone—(dis)entangled. For this reason, others in the House of God and Church of the Living God communities forestall the threat of ambiguity by swearing off nonchurch sacred steel performance, keeping the words it gives and the bodies it moves within the interworld of Holiness-Pentecostal worship.

For his part, Chuck Campbell locates the special powers of his pedal steel in the unusual E9 tuning that was revealed or gifted to him by God. In a conversation with sacred steel scholar Robert Stone, he explains:

> Right, and it had a sound, the country western players didn't like. But it was the most beautiful sounding guitar I've ever had for church. And at that point, what I did then was had an E ninth up top, and I had it and the way I got my tuning, which is from God. You got to be.[7]

Campbell's description of the divine origins and orientation of his tuning brings us to a crossroads of disciplinary possibility where ethnomusicology is not burdened to prove the reality of the secular (the generic and organological genealogies of Campbell's tuning) at the expense of the nonsecular (the sonic/material power of his tuning to bring people into the Holy Spirit). In Amherst, the reality of his tuning being "from God" was as real as the dancing bodies of agnostic clubgoers and Holiness-Pentecostal churchgoers. Ethnomusicological knowing can rest in both those realities. To put a finer point on it, a secular stance that might equate the stereotypical movements of dancing clubgoers and churchgoers is a secular stance that privileges the isomorphism of all E9 tunings—a stance overly committed to the choreosonic evidence of things seen and heard. Along the way, dancers' different relationships with other-than-human agents and the ontological difference of sacred steel gospel and Nashville E9 tunings are lost, to ethnomusicology's detriment.[8] As scholars from McAllester to Hagedorn have shown us, the ethnomusicologically or choreosonically real may not be audible. The musical is not always the sonic. Other-than-human agency, in other words, can precede or be indifferent to its sonic expression.[9] To approach an E9 tuning as universal rather than an epiphenomenon is to capture and enclose in a particular analytical metalanguage that favors scientistic replication, the opposite of decolonizing. The takeaway for our (dis)entangled moment is this: a nonsecular ethnomusicology is not obligated to discount the this-worldly moorings of a sacred steel E9 tuning that saves and anoints (see Campbell's longer narrative in footnote 5), and a secular ethnomusicology might reorient its terms of analysis around a tuning's links to being saved or anointed. The religious affordances of a gamut of frets and pedals, in other words, may be encountered as sound, or maybe not.

Religion's Inaudibility

This brings me to a brief account of what ethnomusicologists can continue contributing to the study of religion. Perhaps paradoxically, much of ethnomusicology's promise in this regard is its sonic encounters with the liquid categories of music/not music, audible/inaudible, and religion/not religion. Although work on music and sound appears frequently in religious studies journals, handbooks, and companions (particularly those devoted to religious media and sensory religion, a core sampling of which I cite in this book), canonical texts surveying religious studies' keywords and commitments tend to give short shrift to ethnomusicology's purview—music, voice, and sound in religious listening, mediation, learning, ritual, conflict, identification, and so on. Combing through the tables of contents and indexes of such work on my desk and online, I find abundant mention of religious images and imagining, texts and temporalities, bodies and embodiments, media and material, vision and touch, space and place, and artifacts both digital and analog, but far less about what ethnomusicology does and far fewer ethnomusicologists in the interdisciplinary mix of scholars.[10]

This may well be due to ethnomusicology's (diminishing but still readily discernible) disciplinary inwardness—attributable, in part, to the observation that, in the anthropologist Michelle Bigenho's words, "music still overwhelms ethnomusicology's project" (2008: 31). And even as ethnomusicology is purportedly defined by its methodologies rather than repertoires, the still-present, intransigent "ethno-" continues to operate according to colonial, colonizing, racializing secular logics that do, in fact, imply a repertoire: ethno- (Schultz 2020). The twinned critiques of ethno- and music are a commonplace, but I hope to have shed some additional light on a disentangled ethnomusicology's contributions and shortcomings and an entangled ethnomusicology's gestures beyond the ethno- and music paradigms here, not least as a way of noting the otherwise futures and disciplinary labels emergent in (dis)entangled scholarship.

In closing, I invite ethnomusicologists and music studies scholars to lean into their methodological strengths to amplify their address beyond their disciplines to scholarship on religion that might gain from a different attention to music and sound.[11] I will concentrate on one example: the trope of other-than-human agents being invisible or unseen as a through line in recent work that rehabilitates the reality of their agency.[12] Marshall Sahlins says this:

> To keep in mind: the "spirits" are real, active co-workers in human economic projects. To consider here: for all their usual invisibility, the spirits are co-present with humans in the same reality. The spirits

> may be invisible to the people, but the people are visible to the spirits. Because they are normally—but not always or necessarily—invisible does not mean they are somewhere else, on some other plane of existence. (2022: 41)

Or Tanya Luhrmann:

> The basic claim is this: *that god or spirit—the invisible other—must be made real for people, and that this real-making changes those who do it.* (2020: xii)

> Gods and spirits are invisible, immaterial, not accessible to the senses in ordinary ways. If humans are to feel the presence of these beings, they must know how to look, how to listen, and how to experience the event. They must learn how to know that spirits respond. (2020: 157)

Or Robert Orsi:

> The unseeing of the gods was an achievement; the challenge is to see them again. (2016: 252)

> Religion is the practice of making the invisible visible [. . .] Once made material, the invisible can be negotiated and bargained with, touched and kissed, made to bear human anger and disappointment. (2005: 73–74)

Setting aside questions of what divine invisibility might mean in Hindu and Buddhist *darśan* or Christian iconography, for instance, and of divine immateriality, what about other-than-humans' audibility? What about aurality in the knowledge of other-than-human realities? My point here is not to rehearse the idealization of listening and hearing in sound studies scholar Jonathan Sterne's "audiovisual litany" (2003: 15),[13] but to return attention to the ethnomusicology I engage with in *Music and Religion*. Throughout the book, ethnomusicologists listen and hear in secular modes that disentangle and nonsecular modes that entangle. Both modalities are, at some level, independent of other-than-human invisibility and the "acousmatic question" (Eidsheim 2018) of sonic sources. This complicates the invisible/unseen trope and the secular boundaries of religion in productive ways. In the Introduction, the praise-singing women at the Mt. Calvary Holy Church Christian Restoration Centre in Nairobi did not relate visually to God, but the Father/Yahweh they sang to was already real, an auditor of their praise and an author of their social/economic relationships. They sang to their Father/Yahweh as they sang to each other; their Father/Yahweh listened as they listened to each other. This braiding of human and other-than-human sonic relationships involves a God who is already real in the women's knowledge and the risks and rewards of chama participation. The audibility of the moment makes it possible to apprehend and attend to other-than-human agency without first having to establish its reality.

Returning from the Mt. Calvary Holy Church Christian Restoration Centre, we encounter other moments of religion's audibility peppered throughout this book, independent of the visibly seen or the voice/sound of an other-than-human being that recording technology may or may not capture:

- Bruno Nettl points to Tyagaraja's profound accomplishments as an outcome of divine beneficence and intervention;
- David McAllester points to the potent dangers of Enemy Way songs' misuse;
- Philip Bohlman points toward intersections of musical ontologies, sonic theologies, and communal identities;
- Gilbert Rouget points to the sonic as the socialization of trance rather than its cause;
- Ethnomusicologists engaged in the "samā' polemic" point to musicologies attuned to listeners' spiritual condition;
- Regula Qureshi points to how ritual economies shape forms of Qawwali performance;
- Jim Sykes points to sonic causality and gifting as necessary frames for religion's audibility beyond the musical;
- Judith Becker points to how a trancer is musicked in a religious habitus of listening irreducible to the sonic or the neurobiological;

- Katherine Hagedorn points to her knowing through initiation as a means of articulating Santería's sonic theology;
- Melvin Butler, Alisha Lola Jones, and Braxton Shelley each point to moments of anointing presence in the choreosonics of gospel-driven worship.

At these moments, ethnomusicology can apprehend and attend to the real, not only the making real, in religion's audibility. And, inconvenient for the secular bracketing of religion, religious musics and sounds can exceed their categorical enclosure, confronting secular reason with the perpetual co-constitution of the religious and the secular. This is a distinction that matters in the work of decolonizing and provincializing religion across disciplines, since it orients us to the human/other-than-human relationships that constitute religion and, incrementally, away from the lingering secular suspicions of their making. Indeed, ethnomusicology's renewed attention to human/other-than-human/material sonic relationships reinforces the fact that those relationships may well not be religious or recognizable as religion, putting added pressure on those terms even as I use them here.

On the other hand, religion's reality may, indeed, be inaudible, and this is another of ethnomusicology's strengths. The movement of The Campbell Brothers' sacred steel guitars from early twentieth-century US-American popular musical spaces into House of God worship may not make those instruments' powers to drive the movement of the Holy Spirit in Holiness-Pentecostal churches audible. Chuck Campbell's E9 tuning "from God" may not be audibly distinct from a standard Nashville E9 tuning. These inaudibilities—along with those of non-vibrational, other-than-human sound and religious sounds to which one is refused universal access—articulate onto-epistemological difference and sovereignty. In encountering religion's inaudibility, ethnomusicology can recognize "the right to opacity" (Glissant 1997: 190), accept invitations to know and not know religious sound otherwise, and continue coming to terms with rebukes of the discipline's colonizing habits.[14] Ultimately, this book is an invitation to continue reading and listening beyond the ethnomusicological story I tell here. Disentangling and entangling matter differently, or not at all, in ethnomusicologies whose secular or nonsecular praxes reflect other commitments and traditions. To the benefit of all music studies, those ethnomusicologies can make strange the moments of disentangling and entangling music and religion that shaped this project.

Notes

1. The pitfalls of a belief-based approach to religious experience hinging on verification—either the Holy Spirit or a charismatic performer, in Becker's case—are part of a broader "earnest turn" in religious studies (Mayblin 2017) that forecloses many of the entanglements I write about here.
2. Schultz describes how this unfolds in *rāṣṭrīya kīrtan*: "Kīrtan's nationalist efficacy owes much to its devotional context, its hagiographical and semi-historical storytelling, and its gestures, but music supplies one of the most important links in the affective chain. Music allows audience members to participate in the kīrtankār's [performer of *kīrtan*] version of religion and/or nationalism, and the eclectic repertoire of song genres can be ordered and contextualized in ways that suggest new modes of identity" (2013: 8).
3. Using the two other terms I interweave throughout *Music and Religion*, "(dis) entangling" can be another signifier of the third thing that characterizes the disciplinary moment I write about here. My point, in the spirit of the relational approach I adopt throughout, is that disentangling and entangling ethnomusicologies and ethnomusicologists are in relationship rather than in binary opposition.
4. For the definitive account of the sacred steel tradition, see Robert Stone's *Sacred Steel: Inside an African American Steel Guitar Tradition* (2010).
5. Video of Darick Campbell performing "A Change Is Gonna Come" is available at https://www.youtube.com/watch?v=SGqaWjw1wyI&t=984s
6. Cf. Crawley, *Blackpentecostal Breath: The Aesthetics of Possibility* (2016); Le Guin, *Boccherini's Body: An Essay in Carnal Musicology* (2005); and Wallace, *King's Vibrato: Modernism, Blackness, and the Sonic Life of Martin Luther King Jr.* (2022).
7. From https://arhoolie.org/sacred-steel-archive-chuck-campbell-interview/. In this same interview, Campbell elaborates on the House of God lineage of his tuning: "I started with . . . . My tuning that I have now, started with . . . Is really a mixture of Ted [Beard]'s tuning, and Calvin [Cooke]'s, and Henry [Nelson]'s. And it evolved into a E ninth top with the bottom being a mixture of those [. . .] Starting from the top is an F, I'm playing a 12-string MSA [. . .] So I have a F# to a Eb to the G# to the E, E7, this is where Calvin's tune come in. I mean the next one after the E is a D that's where Calvin's that's the seventh [. . .] And then I have the B, G sharp, two Es that are tuned exactly the same, this is Calvin's. And then I have a B, another E and a B. And what happened with the . . . I moved from a . . . Let me give you a progression of my guitars, so that'll give you a glimpse of what happened. I went from the six string, to a dual eight. And what everybody wanted at that time was an eight string Fender [. . .] And Ted had the double eight at the time and Calvin had the single eight and I always wanted eight and I finally got an eight, but by that—I went from a double eight Japanese made steel, to an eight string Fender, and then I went to a 10 string double neck white sierra with the Z legs. And that was one pretty box, but it had two cases to carry this thing around there."
8. This is Ana Mariá Ochoa Gautier's point in *Aurality* regarding the entanglement of the ontological and the epistemological (2014: 26).

9. I use indifference here in Naisargi N. Davé's sense of "not desiring *to do anything with*, for, and via the difference of others" (2023: 6).
10. The excellent work I have in mind in making this point includes Hent de Vries's *Religion: Beyond a Concept* (2008); Mark C. Taylor's *Critical Terms for Religious Studies* (1998); Sally M. Promey's *Sensational Religion: Sensory Cultures in Material Practice* (2014); Nickolas P. Roubekas and Robert A. Segal's *The Wiley Blackwell Companion to the Study of Religion* (2017); and Michael Stausberg and Steven Engler's *The Oxford Handbook of the Study of Religion* (2016) and *Routledge Handbook of Research Methods in the Study of Religion* (2022). In religious studies and anthropology, the notable exceptions to this trend are found in the work of Frank Burch Brown (2014), Rosalind I. J. Hackett (2011, 2020), Nicholas Harkness (2025), Leigh Eric Schmidt (2000), and Isaac Weiner (2014).
11. Recent work in this vein includes Dominik Höink and Andreas Meyer's edited volume *Music and Religions in the 21st Century* (2024) (particularly Isabel Laack's [2024] chapter in the same) and Carola Lorea and Rosalind Hackett's edited volume *Religious Sounds Beyond the Global North* (2023) (particularly Carola Lorea's [2023a] chapter in the same).
12. In addition to Sahlins, Luhrmann, and Orsi, also see Meyer and Stordalen (2016), Morgan (2005), and Schielke (2019).
13. Sterne draws attention to the particular Christian and Jewish religious groundings of how sound and orality are privileged in the "audiovisual litany" in his "The Theology of Sound: A Critique of Orality" (2011).
14. This form of inaudibility is a counterpoint to the "zone of the *audible inaudible*" that Martin Daughtry locates in wartime Iraq. That zone is "a conceptual space that housed sounds so distant and/or ubiquitous that they ceased to draw the attention of the experienced auditor" (2015: 77).

Bibliography

Agawu, Kofi. 2023. *On African Music: Techniques, Influences, Scholarship*. New York: Oxford University Press.

Agawu, Kofi. 2003. *Representing African Music: Postcolonial Notes, Queries, Positions*. New York: Routledge.

al Faruqi, Lois Ibsen. 1985. "Music, Musicians and Muslim Law." *Asian Music* 19(1): 2–25.

al Faruqi, Lois Ibsen. 1983. "What Makes 'Religious Music' Religious?" *Sacred Sound: Music in Religious Thought and Practice*. Joyce Irwin, ed. Chico, CA: Scholar's Press, 21–34.

Alter, Andrew. 2019. "Expressing Sonic Theology: Understanding Ritual Action in a Himalayan Festival." *Ethnomusicology Forum* 28(3): 321–337.

Amico, Stephen. 2020. "'We Are All Musicologists Now'; or, the End of Ethnomusicology." *Journal of Musicology* 37(1): 1–32.

An, Yountae. 2024. *The Coloniality of the Secular: Race, Religion, and the Poetics of World- Making*. Durham, NC: Duke University Press.

Asad, Talal. 2003. *Formations of the Secular: Christianity, Islam, Modernity*. Palo Alto: Stanford University Press.

Asad, Talal. 1993. *Genealogies of Religion: Discipline and Reasons of Power in Christianity and Islam*. Baltimore: Johns Hopkins University Press.

Asad, Talal, Wendy Brown, Judith Butler, and Saba Mahmood. 2009. *Is Critique Secular?: Blasphemy, Injury, and Free Speech*. Berkeley: Townsend Papers in the Humanities.

Bakhle, Janaki. 2008. "Music as the Sound of the Secular." *Comparative Studies in Society and History*. 50(1): 256–284.

Bakhle, Janaki. 2005. *Two Men and Music: Nationalism in the Making of an Indian Classical Tradition*. New York: Oxford University Press.

Bakker Kellogg, Sarah. 2025. *Sonic Icons: Relation, Recognition, and Revival in a Syriac World*. New York: Fordham University Press.

Barron, Charisse. 2020. "Bridging Liturgies in the Black Lives Matter Era." *Liturgy* 35(4): 51–57.

Barz, Gregory. 2006. "'We Are from Different Ethnic Groups, but We Live Here as One Family': The Music Performance of Community in a Tanzanian *Kwaya*." *Chorus and Community*. Karen Ahlquist, ed. Urbana: University of Illinois Press, 19–44.

Barz, Gregory. 2005. "Soundscapes of Disaffection and Spirituality in Tanzanian *Kwaya* Music." *The World of Music* 47(1): 5–32.

Barz, Gregory. 2003. *Performing Religion: Negotiating Past and Present in Kwaya Music of Tanzania*. New York: Rodopi.

Barz, Gregory and Timothy J. Cooley, eds. 2008. *Shadows in the Field: New Perspectives for Fieldwork in Ethnomusicology*, second edition. New York: Oxford University Press.

Bates, Eliot. 2019. "Actor-Network Theory and Organology." *Journal of the American Musical Instrument Society* 44: 41–51.

Bates, Eliot. 2012. "The Social Life of Musical Instruments." *Ethnomusicology* 56(3): 363–395.

Bauman, Richard. 1975. "Verbal Art as Performance." *American Anthropologist* 77(2): 290–311.

Beck, Guy L. 2023. *Musicology of Religion: Theories, Methods, and Directions.* Albany: State University of New York Press.

Beck, Guy L. 1993. *Sonic Theology: Hinduism and Sacred Sound.* Columbia, SC: University of South Carolina Press.

Becker, Judith. 2004. *Deep Listeners: Music, Emotion, and Trancing.* Bloomington: Indiana University Press.

Bell, Catherine. 1992. *Ritual Theory, Ritual Practice.* New York: Oxford University Press.

Bennett, Jane. 2010. *Vibrant Matter: A Political Ecology of Things.* Durham, NC: Duke University Press.

Berger, Harris M. and Ruth M. Stone, eds. 2019. *Theory for Ethnomusicology: Histories, Conversations, Insights,* second edition. New York: Routledge.

Berger, Peter. 1967. *The Sacred Canopy: Elements of a Sociological Theory of Religion.* New York: Anchor Books.

Berliner, Paul F. 1994. *Thinking in Jazz: The Infinite Art of Improvisation.* Chicago: University of Chicago Press.

Berliner, Paul F. 1978. *The Soul of Mbira: Music and Traditions of the Shona People of Zimbabwe.* Berkeley: University of California Press.

Bessire, Lucas and David Bond. 2014. "Ontological Anthropology and the Deferral of Critique." *American Ethnologist* 41(3): 440–456.

Bhogal, Gurminder Kaur. 2023. "*Anahad Naad* and Pictorial Resonance: The Halo and Sonic Vibration in Sikh Art." *Sikh Research Journal* 8(1). https://doi.org/10.62307/srj.v8i1.20

Bhogal, Gurminder Kaur. 2017. "Listening to Female Voices in Sikh *Kirtan.*" *Sikh Formations* 13(1–2): 48–77.

Bialecki, Jon. 2014. "Does God Exist in Methodological Atheism? On Tanya Lurhmann's *When God Talks Back* and Bruno Latour." *Anthropology of Consciousness* 25(1): 32–52.

Bielo, James. 2015. *Anthropology of Religion: The Basics.* New York: Routledge.

Bigenho, Michelle. 2008. "Why I'm Not an Ethnomusicologist: A View from Anthropology." *The New (Ethno)musicologies.* Henry Stobart, ed. Lanham, MD: The Scarecrow Press, 28–39.

Binson-Sumrongthong, Bussakorn. 2009. "Rites and Beliefs of Music in the Thailand's Lanna Region." *Fontes Artis Musicae* 56(3): 299–313.

Bissett Perea, Jessica. 2021. *Sound Relations: Native Ways of Doing Music History in Alaska.* Oxford: Oxford University Press.

Bissett Perea, Jessica and Gabriel Solis. 2019. "Asking the Indigeneity Question of American Music Studies." *Journal of the Society for American Music* 13(4): 401–410.

Blacking, John. 1984. "Comment on Tuzin's 'Miraculous Voices: The Auditory Experience of Numinous Objects.'" *Current Anthropology* 25(5): 589–590.

Blacking, John. 1973. *How Musical is Man?* Seattle: University of Washington Press.

Blacking, John. 1971. "Deep and Surface Structures in Venda Music." *Yearbook of the International Folk Music Council* 3: 91–108.

Blanton, Anderson. 2015. *Hittin' the Prayer Bones: Materiality of Spirit in the Pentecostal South.* Chapel Hill, NC: University of North Carolina Press.

Blum, Stephen. 2013. "Foundations of Musical Knowledge in the Muslim World." *The Cambridge History of World Music.* Philip V. Bohlman, ed. Cambridge: Cambridge University Press, 103–124.

Blum, Stephen. 1991. "Prologue: Ethnomusicologists and Modern Music History." *Ethnomusicology and Modern Music History.* Stephen Blum, Philip V. Bohlman, and Daniel M. Neuman, eds. Urbana: University of Illinois Press, 1–20.

Bohlman, Philip V. 2018. "Musical Thought in the Global Enlightenments." *Studies on a Global History of Music: A Balzan Musicology Project.* Reinhard Strohm, ed. New York: Routledge, 61–80.

Bohlman, Philip V. 2008. *Jewish Music and Modernity.* New York: Oxford University Press.

Bohlman, Philip V. 1999. "Ontologies of Music." *Rethinking Music.* Nicholas Cook and Mark Everist, eds. New York: Oxford University Press, 17–34.

Bohlman, Philip V. 1997. "World Musics and World Religions: *Whose World*?" *Enchanting Powers: Music in the World's Religions.* Lawrence E. Sullivan, ed. Cambridge, MA: Harvard Center for the Study of World Religions, 61–90.

Bohlman, Philip V. 1994 [1989]. "Is All Music Religious? *Black Sacred Music* 8(1): 3–12.

Bohlman, Philip V. and Jeffers Engelhardt. 2016. "Resounding Transcendence—An Introduction." *Resounding Transcendence: Transitions in Music, Religion, and Ritual.* Jeffers Engelhardt and Philip V. Bohlman, eds. New York: Oxford University Press, 1–28.

Bouteneff, Peter C., Jeffers Engelhardt, and Rober Saler, eds. 2021. *Arvo Pärt: Sounding the Sacred.* New York: Fordham University Press.

Boyer, Horace Clarence. 1979. "Contemporary Gospel Music." *The Black Perspective in Music* 7(1): 5–58.

Brabec de Mori, Bernd. 2017. "Music and Non-Human Agency." *Ethnomusicology: A Contemporary Reader,* volume 2. Jennifer Post, ed. New York: Routledge, 181–194.

Brabec de Mori, Bernd. 2015. "Sonic Substances and Silent Sounds: An Auditory Anthropology of Ritual Songs." *Tipití: Journal of the Society of the Anthropology of Lowland South America* 13(2): 25–43.

Brown, Frank Burch, ed. 2014. *The Oxford Handbook of Religion and the Arts.* New York: Oxford University Press.

Burnim, Mellonee. 1985. "Culture Bearer and Tradition Bearer: An Ethnomusicologist's Research on Gospel Music." *Ethnomusicology* 29(3): 432–447.

Burnim, Mellonee. 1983. "Gospel Music: Review of the Literature." *Music Educators Journal* 69(9): 58–61.

Butler, Melvin L. 2023. "Playful Transcendence: Paths to Human Flourishing in Black Music Research and Performing." *Music & Human Flourishing.* Anna Harwell Celenza, ed. New York: Oxford University Press, 175–197.

Butler, Melvin L. 2021. "Researching Black Congregational Music from a Migratory Point of View: Methods, Challenges, and Strategies." *Studying Congregational*

Music: Key Issues, Methods, and Theoretical Perspectives. Andrew Mall, Jeffers Engelhardt, and Monique M. Ingalls, eds. New York: Routledge, 174–192.

Butler, Melvin L. 2019. *Island Gospel: Pentecostal Music and Identity in Jamaica and the United States*. Urbana: University of Illinois Press.

Butler, Melvin L. 2016. "Performing Pannkotis Identity in Haiti." *The Oxford Handbook of Music and World Christianities*. Suzel Ana Reily and Jonathan Dueck, eds. New York: Oxford University Press, 606–628.

Butler, Melvin L. 2014. "Singing Like David Sang: Queerness and Masculinity in Black Gospel Performance." *Readings in African American Music and Worship, Volume 2*. James Abbington, ed. Chicago: GIA Publications, 715–725.

Butler, Melvin L. 2008a. "In Zora's Footsteps: Experiencing Music and Pentecostal Ritual in the African Diaspora." *Obsidian* 9(1): 74–106.

Butler, Melvin L. 2008b. "The Weapons of Our Warfare: Music, Positionality, and Transcendence among Haitian Pentecostals." *Caribbean Studies* 36(2): 23–64.

Butler, Melvin L. 2002. "'Nou Kwe nan Sentespri' (We Believe in the Holy Spirit): Music, Ecstasy, and Identity in Haitian Pentecostal Worship." *Black Music Research Journal* 22(1): 85–125.

Butler, Melvin L. 2000. "Musical Style and Experience in a Brooklyn Pentecostal Church: An 'Insider's' Perspective." *Current Musicology* 70: 33–50.

Cannell, Fenella. 2005. "The Christianity of Anthropology." *Journal of the Royal Anthropological Institute* 11(2): 335–356.

Casanova, José. 1994. *Public Religions in the Modern World*. Chicago: University of Chicago Press.

Cassaniti, Julia L. and Tanya Marie Luhrmann. 2014. "The Cultural Kindling of Spiritual Experiences." *Current Anthropology* 55(S10): S333–S343.

Castro-Gómez, Santiago. 2021. *Zero-Point Hubris: Science, Race, and Enlightenment in Eighteenth-Century Latin America*. George Ciccariello-Maher and Don T. Deere, trans. Lanham, MD: Rowman & Littlefield.

Chakrabarty, Dipesh. 2000. *Provincializing Europe: Postcolonial Thought and Historical Difference*. Princeton: Princeton University Press.

Chatterjee, Sebanti. 2023. *Choral Voices: Ethnographic Imaginations of Sound and Sacrality*. New York: Bloomsbury.

Chen, Jen-yen. 2021. "Institutional Religion and Personal Religiosity in a Postcolonial Context: Sacred Music and the Chinese Catholic Community in Contemporary Macau." *Acta Musicologica* 93(2): 199–218.

Chen, Pi-yen. 2001. "Sound and Emptiness: Music, Philosophy, and the Monastic Practice of Buddhist Doctrine." *History of Religions* 41(1): 24–48.

Chen, Pi-yen, ed. 2010. 梵唄 *Chinese Buddhist Monastic Chants*. Middleton, WI: A-R Editions.

Chernoff, John Miller. 1979. *African Rhythm and African Sensibility: Aesthetics and Social Action in African Musical Idioms*. Chicago: University of Chicago Press.

Chidester, David. 2014. *Empire of Religion: Imperialism and Comparative Religion*. Chicago: University of Chicago Press.

Clayton, Martin, Trevor Herbert, and Richard Middleton, eds. 2012. *The Cultural Study of Music: A Critical Introduction*, second edition. New York: Routledge.

Clifford, James and George E. Marus, eds. 1986. *Writing Culture: The Poetics and Politics of Ethnography*. Berkeley: University of California Press.

Coleman, Simon. 2022. "Laterality: A Sideways Look at Ritual." *Journal of the Royal Anthropological Institute* 29(4): 727–744.

Crawley, Ashon T. 2016. *Blackpentecostal Breath: The Aesthetics of Possibility.* New York: Fordham University Press.

da Col, Giovanni and David Graeber. 2011. "Foreword: The Return of Ethnographic Theory." *HAU: Journal of Ethnographic Theory* 1(1): vi–xxxv.

Dargan, William T. 1982. *Traditional Gospel Songs in a Black Apostolic-Pentecostal Congregation: A Musical and Textual Analysis.* Ph.D. dissertation, Wesleyan University.

Daughtry, J. Martin. 2015. *Listening to War: Sound, Music, Trauma, and Survival in Wartime Iraq.* New York: Oxford University Press.

Davé, Naisargi N. 2023. *Indifference: On the Praxis of Interspecies Being.* Durham, NC: Duke University Press.

de Vries, Hent, ed. 2008. *Religion: Beyond a Concept.* New York: Fordham University Press.

Deegalle, Mahinda. 2022. "Aural Practices of Chanting and Protection." *The Oxford Handbook of Buddhist Practice.* Kevin Trainor and Paula Arai, eds. New York: Oxford University Press, 301–320.

Descola, Phillipe. 2013. *Beyond Nature and Culture.* Janet Lloyd, trans. Chicago: University of Chicago Press.

Diamond, Beverley. 2013. "Native American Ways of (Music) History." *The Cambridge History of World Music.* Philip V. Bohlman, ed. Cambridge: Cambridge University Press, 155–180.

Diao, Ying. 2023. *Faith by Aurality in China's Ethnic Borderland: Media, Mobility, and Christianity at the Margins.* Rochester, NY: University of Rochester Press.

Dirksen, Rebecca. 2019. "Haiti's Drums and Trees: Facing Loss of the Sacred." *Ethnomusicology* 63(1): 43–77.

DjeDje, Jacqueline Cogdell. 1978. *American Black Spiritual and Gospel Songs from Southeast Georgia: A Comparative Study.* Los Angeles: Center for Afro-American Studies, University of California.

Dole, Andrew C. 2024. "The Vagueness of Religion." *Journal of the American Academy of Religion* 91(4): 757–776.

Douglas, Gavin. 2020. "Metta, Mudita, and Metal: Dhamma Instruments in Burmese Buddhism." *Yale Journal of Music & Religion* 6(1): article 1. https://doi.org/10.17132/2377-231X.1159

Droogers, Andres. 1999. "The Third Bank of the River: Play, Methodological Ludism, and the Definition of Religion." *Conflicts in Social Science.* Anton van Harskamp, ed. New York: Routledge, 44–67.

Dueck, Byron and Essele Essele Kisito. 2022. "Authority, Deference, and Disregard in Catholic Liturgical Music in Central Cameroon." *Ethnomusicology* 66(1): 21–50.

Dumont, Louis. 1970. *Homo Hierarchicus: The Caste System and Its Implications.* Mark Sainsbury, trans. London: Weidenfeld & Nicolson.

During, Jean. 1988. *Musique et extase: l'audition mystique dans la tradition soufie.* Paris: Albin Michel.

Eidsheim, Nina Sun. 2018. *The Race of Sound: Listening, Timbre, and Vocality in African American Music.* Durham, NC: Duke University Press.

Eisenlohr, Patrick. 2024. "Sonic Religion: The Analysis of Atmospheric Half-Things." *Routledge Handbook of Material Religion*. Pooyan Tamimi Arab, Jennifer Scheper-Hughes and S. Brent Rodríguez-Plate, eds. New York: Routledge, 400–410.

Eisenlohr, Patrick. 2018. *Sounding Islam: Voice, Media, and Sonic Atmospheres in an Indian Ocean World*. Berkeley: University of California Press.

El Hadidi, Hager. 2022. *Zar: Sprit Possession, Music, and Healing Rituals in Egypt*. New York: The American University in Cairo Press.

Engelhardt, Jeffers. 2015. *Singing the Right Way: Orthodox Christians and Secular Enchantment in Estonia*. New York: Oxford University Press.

Engelhardt, Jeffers. 2012. "Music, Sound, and Religion." *The Cultural Study of Music: A Critical Introduction*, second edition. Martin Clayton, Trevor Herbert, and Richard Middleton, eds. New York: Routledge, 299–307.

Engelhardt, Jeffers. 2009. "Right Singing in Estonian Orthodox Christianity: A Study of Music, Theology, and Religious Ideology." *Ethnomusicology* 53(1): 32–57.

Engelhardt, Jeffers and Philip V. Bohlman, eds. 2016. *Resounding Transcendence: Transitions in Music, Religion, and Ritual*. New York: Oxford University Press.

Engelhardt, Jeffers and Katherine Pukinskis, eds. 2024. *Baltic Musics Beyond the Post-Soviet*. Tartu: University of Tartu Press.

Engelhardt, Jeffers, Kate Bancroft, Alex Rule, and Charlotte Wang. 2022. "Chorality's Sonic-Social Relationships." *Resonance: The Journal of Sound and Culture* 3(1): 76–97.

Ewing, Katherine P. 1994. "Dreams from a Saint: Anthropological Atheism and the Temptation to Believe." *American Anthropologist* 96(3): 571–583.

Fabian, Johannes. 1983. *Time and the Other: How Anthropology Makes Its Object*. New York: Columbia University Press.

Farmer, Henry George. 1952. "The Religious Music of Islam." *Journal of the Royal Asiatic Society of Great Britain and Ireland* 1(2): 160–165.

Feld, Steven. 1984. "Sound Structure as Social Structure." *Ethnomusicology* 28(3): 383–409.

Feld, Steven. 1982. *Sound and Sentiment: Birds, Weeping, Poetics, and Song in Kaluli Expression*. Philadelphia: University of Pennsylvania Press.

Fink, Robert. 2018. "Below 100 Hz: Toward a Musicology of Bass Culture." *The Relentless Pursuit of Tone: Timbre in Popular Music*. Robert Fink, Melinda Latour, and Zachary Wallmark, eds. New York: Oxford University Press, 88–118.

Friedson, Steven. 2009. *The Remains of Ritual: Northern Gods in a Southern Land*. Chicago: University of Chicago Press.

Friedson, Steven. 1996. *Dancing Prophets: Musical Experience in Tumbuka Healing*. Chicago: University of Chicago Press.

Frigyesi, Judit Niran. 2018. *Writing on Water: The Sounds of Jewish Prayer*. New York: Central European Press.

Furani, Khaled. 2019. *Redeeming Anthropology: A Theological Critique of a Modern Science*. New York: Oxford University Press.

Garvey, Bradford J. 2020. "Warfare and Welcome: Practicality and Qur'ānic Hierarchy in Ibāḍī Muslims' Jurisprudential Rulings on Music." *Yale Journal of Music & Religion* 6(1). https://doi.org/10.17132/2377-231X.1167

Garzoli, John and Tharanat Hin-on. 2023. "Thai Musicology in Context: Epistemic Disparities in Thai and Western Ways of Knowing Thai Music." *Ethnomusicology Forum* 32(2): 224–250.

Geertz, Clifford. 1968. *Islam Observed: Religious Development in Morocco and Indonesia.* Chicago: University of Chicago Press.

Geertz, Clifford. 1966. "Religion as a Cultural System." *Anthropological Approaches to the Study of Religion.* Michael Banton, ed. London: Tavistock, 1–46.

Gell, Alfred. 1998. *Art and Agency: An Anthropological Theory.* New York: Oxford University Press.

Gerety, Finnian M. M. 2021. "Between Sound and Silence in Early Yoga: Meditation on 'Om' at Death." *History of Religions* 60(3): 209–244.

Gerety, Finnian M. M. 2020. "Sound and Yoga." *Routledge Handbook of Yoga and Meditation Studies.* Suzanne Newcombe and Karen O'Brien-Kop, eds. New York: Routledge, 502–521.

Gerety, Finnian M. M. 2016. "Melody, Mantra, and Meaninglessness: Towards a History of OM." *On Meaning and Mantras: Essays in Honor of Frits Staal.* George Thompson and Richard Payne, eds. Moraga, CA: Institute of Buddhist Studies and BDK America, 185–225.

Gerson-Kiwi, Edith. 1961. "Religious Chant: A Pan-Asiatic Conception of Music." *Journal of the International Folk Music Council* 13: 64–67.

Gidal, Marc. 2016. *Spirit Song: Afro-Brazilian Religious Music and Boundaries.* New York: Oxford University Press.

Glissant, Édouard. 1997. *Poetics of Relation.* Betsy Wing, trans. Ann Arbor: University of Michigan Press.

Goshadze, Mariam. 2025. *The Noise Silence Makes: Secularity and Ghana's Drum Wars.* Durham, NC: Duke University Press.

Graeber, David. 2015. "Radical Alterity is Just Another Way of Saying 'Reality': A Reply to Eduardo Viveiros de Castro." *HAU: Journal of Ethnographic Theory* 5(2): 1–41.

Greene, Paul D., Keith Howard, Terry Miller, Phong T. Nguyen, and Hwee-San Tan. 2002. "Buddhism and the Musical Cultures of Asia: A Critical Literature Survey." *The World of Music* 44(2): 135–175.

Gribetz, Arthur. 1991. "The Samā' Controversy: Sufi vs. Legalist." *Studia Islamica* 74: 43–62.

Hackett, Rosalind I. J. 2020. "Aural Media." *The Wiley Blackwell Companion to Religion and Materiality.* Vasudha Narayanan, ed. Hoboken, NJ: Wiley-Blackwell, 487–505.

Hackett, Rosalind I. J. 2011. "Auditory Materials." *Handbook of Research Methods in Religious Studies.* Michael Stausberg and Steven Engler, eds. New York: Routledge, 447–458.

Hagedorn, Katherine J. 2017. "'Where the Transcendent Breaks into Time': Toward a Theology of Sound in Afro-Cuban Regla de Ochá." *Theorizing Sound Writing.* Deborah Kapchan, ed. Middletown: Wesleyan University Press, 216–232.

Hagedorn, Katherine J. 2006. "Toward a Theology of Sound: Drum Talk, Oricha Worship, and Other Ecstatic Phenomena." *Harvard Divinity Bulletin,* Spring 2006. https://bulletin.hds.harvard.edu/toward-a-theology-of-sound/

Hagedorn, Katherine J. 2001. *Divine Utterances: The Performance of Afro-Cuban Santeria*. Washington, DC: Smithsonian Institution.

Halverson, Jeffry R. 2024. "Religion before the Academy: Jonathan Z. Smith, Eurocentrism, and Muslim Demarcations of Religion." *The Journal of Religion* 104(1): 26–44.

Harkness, Nicholas. 2025. "Sound." *Critical Terms for Religious Studies*, second edition. Sarah Hammerschlag, ed. Chicago: University of Chicago Press, 387–402.

Harkness, Nicholas. 2014. *Songs of Seoul: An Ethnography of Voice and Voicing in Christian South Korea*. Berkeley: University of California Press.

Harnish, David D. and Anne K. Rasmussen, eds. 2011. *Divine Inspirations: Music and Islam in Indonesia*. New York: Oxford University Press.

Harris, Rachel. 2020. *Soundscapes of Uyghur Islam*. Bloomington: Indiana University Press.

Harrison, Frank. 1973. *Time, Place, and Music: An Anthology of Ethnomusicological Observations c. 1550 to c. 1800*. Amsterdam: Frits Knuf.

Herndon, Marcia. 1993. "Insiders, Outsiders: Knowing Our Limits, Limiting Our Knowing." *The World of Music* 35(1): 63–80.

Herndon, Marcia and Norma McLeod. 1980. *Music as Culture*. Norwood, PA: Norwood Editions.

Hirschkind, Charles. 2015. "Religion." *Keywords in Sound*. David Novak and Matt Sakakeeny, eds. Durham, NC: Duke University Press, 165–174.

Hirschkind, Charles. 2006. *The Ethical Soundscape: Cassette Sermons and Islamic Counterpublics*. New York: Columbia University Press.

Hoffmann, Anette. 2024. *Knowing by Ear: Listening to Voice Recordings with African Prisoners of War in German Camps (1915–1918)*. Durham, NC: Duke University Press.

Höink, Dominik and Andreas Meyer, eds. 2024. *Music and Religions in the 21st Century*. Baden-Baden: Nomos Wissenschaftsverlag.

Hood, Mantle. 1971. *The Ethnomusicologist*. New York: McGraw-Hill.

Hood, Mantle. 1960. "The Challenge of 'Bi-Musicality.'" *Ethnomusicology* 4(2): 55–59.

Hunt, Lynn, Margaret Jacob, and Wijnand Mijnhardt. 2010a. *The Book that Changed Europe: Picart & Bernard's* Religious Ceremonies of the World. Cambridge, MA: Harvard University Press.

Hunt, Lynn and Margaret Jacob. 2010b. "Introduction." *Bernard Picart and the First Global Vision of Religion*. Lynn Hunt, Margaret Jacob, and Wijnand Mijnhardt, eds. Los Angeles: The Getty Research Institute, 1–13.

Hunter, Cory. 2022. "Thy Kingdom Come: Racial-Ethnic Oneness in African American Gospel Music." *The Musical Quarterly* 105(1/2): 7–43.

Hurston, Zora Neale. 2009 [1938]. *Tell My Horse: Voodoo and Life in Haiti and Jamaica*. New York: Amistad.

Ingalls, Monique M. 2018. *Singing the Congregation: How Contemporary Worship Music Forms Evangelical Community*. New York: Oxford University Press.

Irving, David R. M. 2024. *The Making of European Music in the Long Eighteenth Century*. New York: Oxford University Press.

Jankowsky, Richard C. 2021. *Ambient Sufism: Ritual Niches and the Social Work of Musical Form*. Chicago: University of Chicago Press.

Jankowsky, Richard C. 2010. *Stambeli: Music, Trance, and Alterity in Tunisia.* Chicago: University of Chicago Press.

Jankowsky, Richard C. 2007. "Music, Spirit Possession and the In-between: Ethnomusicological Inquiry and the Challenge of Trance." *Ethnomusicology Forum* 16(2): 185–208.

Jones, Alisha Lola. 2020. *Flaming?: The Peculiar Theopolitics of Fire and Desire in Black Male Gospel Performance.* New York: Oxford University Press.

Jones, Jaime. 2013. "Music, History, and the Sacred in South Asia." *The Cambridge History of World Music.* Philip V. Bohlman, ed. Cambridge: Cambridge University Press, 202–222.

Kalra, Virinder S. 2015. *Sacred and Secular Musics: A Postcolonial Approach.* New York: Bloomsbury.

Kapchan, Deborah. 2007. *Traveling Spirit Masters: Moroccan Gnawa Trance and Music in the Global Marketplace.* Middletown: Wesleyan University Press.

Kärjä, Antti-Ville. 2022. *The Popular and the Sacred in Music.* New York: Routledge.

Kaur, Inderjit N. 2021a. "Theorizing the (Un)Sounded in Sikhī: Anhad, Sabad, and Kīrtan." *Religions* 12(11). https://doi.org/10.3390/rel12111007

Kaur, Inderjit N. 2021b. "Toward a Phenomenology of *Rasa*: Theorizing from *Ras* in Sikh Sabad Kīrtan Practice." *The Oxford Handbook of the Phenomenology of Music Cultures.* Harris M. Berger, Friedlind Riedel, and David VanderHamm, eds. New York: Oxford University Press. https://doi.org/10.1093/oxfordhb/9780190693879.013.19

Kaur, Inderjit N. 2016. "Multiple Authenticities in Motion: Styles and Stances in Sikh Sabad Kīrtan." *Yearbook for Traditional Music.* 48: 71–93.

Keyes, Cheryl L. 2009. "Sound, Voice, and Spirit: Teaching in the Black Music Vernacular." *Black Music Research Journal* 29(1): 11–24.

Kligman, Mark L. 2009. *Maqām and Liturgy: Ritual, Music, and Aesthetics of Syrian Jews in Brooklyn.* Detroit: Wayne State University Press.

Kolar, Miriam A. 2020. "Conch Calls into the Anthropocene: *Pututus* as Instruments of Human-Environmental Relations at Monumental Chavín." *Yale Journal of Music & Religion* 5(2). https://doi.org/10.17132/2377-231X.1151

Korkmaz, Harun and Martin Stokes. 2024. "Islam and Music in Turkey." *The Oxford Handbook of Religion in Turkey.* Caroline Tee, Fabio Vicini, and Philip Dorroll, eds. New York: Oxford University Press. https://doi.org/10.1093/oxfordhb/9780197624883.013.19

Kuang, Lanlan. 2019. "(Un)consciousness?: Music in the Daoist Context of Nonbeing." *Music and Consciousness 2: Worlds, Practices, Modalities.* Ruth Herbert, David Clarke, and Eric Clarke, eds. New York: Oxford University Press, 306–323.

Laack, Isabel. 2024. "Music and Religions in the 21st Century: Perspectives from the Cultural Study of Religion." *Music and Religions in the 21st Century.* Dominik Höink and Andreas Meyer, eds. Baden-Baden: Nomos Wissenschaftsverlag, 7–25.

Laack, Isabel. 2015. "Sound, Music and Religion: A Preliminary Cartography of a Transdisciplinary Research Field." *Method & Theory in the Study of Religion* 27(3): 220–246.

Lambek, Michael. 2008. "Provincializing God?: Provocations from an Anthropology of Religion." *Religion: Beyond a Concept*. Hent de Vries, ed. New York: Fordham University Press, 120–138.

Latour, Bruno. 1993. *We Have Never Been Modern*. Catherine Porter, trans. Cambridge, MA: Harvard University Press.

Le Guin, Elisabeth. 2005. *Boccherini's Body: An Essay in Carnal Musicology*. Berkeley: University of California Press.

Lemons, J. Derrick. 2018. *Theologically Engaged Anthropology*. New York: Oxford University Press.

Lewisohn, Leonard. 1997. "The Sacred Music of Islam: Samā' in the Persian Sufi Tradition." *British Journal of Ethnomusicology* 6: 1–33.

Lomax, Alan. 1976. *Cantometrics: An Approach to the Anthropology of Music*. Berkeley: University of California Extension Media Center.

Lomax, Alan. 1968. *Folk Song Style and Culture*. Washington, DC: American Association for the Advancement of Science.

Lorea, Carola Erika. 2023a. "Introduction: The Potential of a Sonic Turn: Toward an Acoustemology of the Post-Secular." *Religious Sounds Beyond the Global North*. Carola E. Lorea and Rosalind I. J. Hackett, eds. Amsterdam: Amsterdam University Press, 19–60.

Lorea, Carola Erika. 2023b. "An Untouchable Kīrtan: Sonic Liberation on the Andaman Islands." *Sounding the Indian Ocean: Musical Circulations in the Afro-Asiatic Seascape*. Jim Sykes and Julia Byl, eds. Berkeley: University of California Press, 99–119.

Lorea, Carola E. and Rosalind I. J. Hackett, eds. 2023. *Religious Sounds Beyond the Global North*. Amsterdam: Amsterdam University Press.

Lucas, Ann E. 2012. "Caught between Heaven and Hell: The Morality of Music and Cosmologies of the Past in Persian Writings on Listening, c. 1040-c. 1800." *Asian Music* 43(1): 91–130.

Luhrmann, Tanya. M. 2023. "Anthropology as Spiritual Discipline." *American Ethnologist* 51(1): 24–27.

Luhrmann, Tanya. M. 2020. *How God Becomes Real: Kindling the Presence of Invisible Others*. Princeton: Princeton University Press.

Luhrmann, Tanya. M. 2012. *When God Talks Back: Understanding the American Evangelical Relationship with God*. New York: Knopf.

Mabbett, Ian W. 1993. "Buddhism and Music." *Asian Music* 25(1/2): 9–28.

Mahmood, Saba. 2005. *Politics of Piety: The Islamic Revival and the Feminist Subject*. Princeton: Princeton University Press.

Mall, Andrew. 2021. *God Rock, Inc.: The Business of Niche Music*. Berkeley: University of California Press.

Mall, Andrew, Jeffers Engelhardt, and Monique M. Ingalls, eds. 2021. *Studying Congregational Music: Key Issues, Methods, and Theoretical Perspectives*. New York: Routledge.

Masuzawa, Tomoko. 2005. *The Invention of World Religions: Or, How European Universalism Was Preserved in the Language of Pluralism*. Chicago: University of Chicago Press.

Maultsby, Portia K. 1992. "The Impact of Gospel Music on the Secular Music Industry." *We'll Understand It Better By and By: Pioneering African American*

Gospel Composers. Bernice Johnson Reagon, ed. Washington, DC: Smithsonian Institution, 19–33.

Maultsby, Portia K. 1983. "The Use and Performance of Hymnody, Spirituals, and Gospels in the Black Church." *Western Journal of Black Studies* 7(3): 161–171.

Mayblin, Maya. 2017. "The Lapsed and the Laity: Discipline and Lenience in the Study of Religion." *Journal of the Royal Anthropological Institute* 23(3): 503–522.

Mbembe, Achille. 2016. "Decolonizing the University: New Directions." *Arts and Humanities in Higher Education* 15(1): 29–45.

McAllester, David P. 1954. *Enemy Way Music: A Study of Social and Esthetic Values as Seen in Navaho Music*. Cambridge, MA: Peabody Museum.

Meadows, Ruthie. 2023. *Efficacy of Sound: Power, Potency, and Promise in the Translocal Ritual Music of Cuban Ifá-Òrìṣà*. Chicago: University of Chicago Press.

Meizel, Katherine and J. Martin Daughtry. 2019. "Decentering Music: Sound Studies and Voice Studies in Ethnomusicology." *Theory for Ethnomusicology: Histories, Conversations, Insights*. Harris Berger and Ruth Stone, eds. New York: Routledge, 176–203.

Meneses, Eloise and David Bronkema, eds. 2017. *On Knowing Humanity: Insights from Theology for Anthropology*. New York: Routledge.

Merriam, Alan P. 1964. *The Anthropology of Music*. Evanston: Northwestern University Press.

Merriam, Alan P. 1961. "Death and the Religious Philosophy of the Basongye." *The Antioch Review* 21(3): 293–304.

Meyer, Birgit. 2011. "Mediation and Immediacy: Sensational Forms, Semiotic Ideologies, and the Question of the Medium." *Social Anthropology* 19(1): 23–39.

Meyer, Birgit. 2009. "Introduction: From Imagined Communities to Aesthetic Formations: Religious Mediations, Sensational Forms, and Styles of Binding." *Aesthetic Formations: Media, Religion, and the Senses*. Birgit Meyer, ed. New York: Palgrave Macmillan, 1–28.

Meyer, Birgit and Terje Stordalen, eds. 2019a. *Figurations and Sensations of the Unseen in Judaism, Christianity, and Islam: Contested Desires*. New York: Bloomsbury Academic.

Meyer, Birgit and Terje Stordalen. 2019b. "Introduction: Figurations and Sensations of the Unseen in Judaism, Christianity, and Islam." *Figurations and Sensations of the Unseen in Judaism, Christianity, and Islam: Contested Desires*. New York: Bloomsbury Academic, 1–18.

Mittermaier, Amira. 2021. "Beyond the Human Horizon." *Religion and Society* 12(1): 21–38.

Moll, Yasmin. 2023. "Can There Be a Godly Ethnography? Islamic Anthropology, Epistemic Decolonization, and the Ethnographic Stance." *American Anthropologist* 125(4): 1–15.

Moore, Robin D. 2018. *Fernando Ortiz on Music: Selected Writing on Afro-Cuban Culture*. Philadelphia: Temple University Press.

Morgan, David. 2005. *The Sacred Gaze: Religious Visual Culture in Theory and Practice*. Berkeley: University of California Press.

Narayan, Kirin. 2016. *Everyday Creativity: Singing Goddesses in the Himalayan Foothills*. Chicago: University of Chicago Press.

Nasr, Seyyed Hossein. 1997. "Islam and Music: The Legal and Spiritual Dimensions." *Enchanting Powers: Music in the World's Religions*. Lawrence E. Sullivan, ed. Cambridge, MA: Harvard Center for the Study of World Religions, 219–236.

Needham, Rodney. 1967. "Percussion and Transition." *Man* 2(4): 606–614.

Neusner, Jacob. 1995. *Judaism's Theological Voice: The Melody of the Talmud*. Chicago: University of Chicago Press.

Nelson, Kristina. 1985. *The Art of Reciting the Qur'an*. Austin: University of Texas Press.

Nettl, Bruno. 2015. *The Study of Ethnomusicology: Thirty-Three Discussions*, third edition. Urbana: University of Illinois Press.

Nettl, Bruno. 2013. "On World Music as a Concept in the History of Music Scholarship." *The Cambridge History of World Music*. Philip V. Bohlman, ed. Cambridge: Cambridge University Press, 23–54.

Nettl, Bruno. 2010. *Nettl's Elephant: On the History of Ethnomusicology*. Urbana: University of Illinois Press.

Nettl, Bruno. 1964. *Theory and Method in Ethnomusicology*. New York: Free Press of Glencoe.

Ochoa Gautier, Anna María. 2014. *Aurality: Listening and Knowledge in Nineteenth-Century Colombia*. Durham, NC: Duke University Press.

Ochoa Gautier, Anna María. 2006. "Sonic Transculturation, Epistemologies of Purification and the Aural Public Sphere in Latin America." *Social Identities* 12(6): 803–825.

Orsi, Robert A. 2016. *History and Presence*. Cambridge, MA: Harvard University Press.

Orsi, Robert A. 2005. *Between Heaven and Earth: The Religious Worlds People Make and the Scholars Who Study Them*. Princeton: Princeton University Press.

Palmié, Stephan. 2023. *Thinking with Ngangas: What Afro-Cuban Ritual Can Tell Us About Scientific Practice and Vice Versa*. Chicago: University of Chicago Press.

Pavez Ojeda, Jorge. 2021. "The Fetishes of Fernando Ortiz." *HAU: Journal of Ethnographic Theory* 11(1): 122–140.

Pegg, Carole. 2001. "Introduction: Ethnomusicology." *Grove Music Online*. https://doi.org/10.1093/gmo/9781561592630.article.52178

Picart, Bernard and Jean-Frédéric Bernard Bernard. 1733–1739 [1723–37]. *The Ceremonies and Religious Customs of the Various Nations of the Known World; together with historical annotations and several curious discourses. Written originally in French, and illustrated with a large number of folio copper plates designed by Mr. Bernard Picart, and curiously engraved by most of the best hands in Europe*. 7 volumes. London: William Jackson and Claude Dubosc.

Pickering, Andrew. 2017. "The Ontological Turn: Taking Different Worlds Seriously." *Social Analysis* 61(2): 134–150.

Piekut, Benjamin. 2014. "Actor-Networks in Music History: Clarifications and Critiques." *Twentieth-Century Music* 11(2): 191–215.

Pohran, Nadya. 2022. "Belief-Inclusive Research: Does Strategically 'Bracketing Out' a Researcher's (Religious) Beliefs and Doubts Limit Access to Ethnographic Data?" *Current Anthropology* 63(6): 691–713.

Promey, Sally M., ed. 2014. *Sensational Religion: Sensory Cultures in Material Practice*. New Haven: Yale University Press.

Qing, Tian and Tan Hwee San. 1994. "Recent Trends in Buddhist Music Research in China." *British Journal of Ethnomusicology* 3: 63–72.

Qureshi, Regula Burckhardt. 1999. "Other Musicologies: Exploring Issues and Confronting Practice in India." *Rethinking Music.* Nicholas Cook and Mark Everist, eds. New York: Oxford University Press, 311–335.

Qureshi, Regula Burckhardt. 1995 [1986]. *Sufi Music of India and Pakistan: Sound, Context, and Meaning in Qawwali.* Chicago: University of Chicago Press.

Qureshi, Regula Burckhardt. 1972. "Indo-Muslim Religious Music, an Overview." *Asian Music* 3(2): 15–22.

Racy, Ali Jihad. 1991. *Making Music in the Arab World: The Culture and Artistry of Tarab.* Cambridge: Cambridge University Press.

Ramsey, Guthrie P., Jr. 2003. *Race Music: Black Cultures from Bebop to Hip-Hop.* Berkeley: University of California Press.

Rappaport, Roy. 1999. *Ritual and Religion in the Making of Humanity.* Cambridge: Cambridge University Press.

Rasmussen, Anne K. 2010. *Women, the Recited Qur'an, and Islamic Music in Indonesia.* Berkeley: University of California Press.

Reed, Teresa L. 2012. "Shared Possessions: Black Pentecostals, Afro-Caribbeans, and Sacred Music." *Black Music Research Journal* 32(1): 5–25.

Reed, Teresa L. 2003. *The Holy Profane: Religion in Black Popular Music.* Lexington, KY: The University Press of Kentucky.

Reily, Suzel Ana. 2002. *Voices of the Magi: Enchanted Journeys in Southeast Brazil.* Chicago: University of Chicago Press.

Reily, Suzel Ana and Jonathan M. Dueck. 2016. "Introduction." *The Oxford Handbook of Music and World Christianities.* Suzel Ana Reily and Jonathan M. Dueck, eds. New York: Oxford University Press, 1–32.

Rice, Timothy. 2017. *Modeling Ethnomusicology.* New York: Oxford University Press.

Robbins, Joel. 2020. *Theology and the Anthropology of Christian Life.* New York: Oxford University Press.

Robinson, Dylan. 2020. *Hungry Listening: Resonant Theory for Indigenous Sound Studies.* Minneapolis: University of Minnesota Press.

Roda, R. Allen. 2014. "Tabla Tuning on the Workshop Stage: Toward a Materialist Musical Ethnography." *Ethnomusicology Forum* 23(3): 360–382.

Rommen, Timothy. 2007. *Mek Some Noise: Gospel Music and the Ethics of Style in Trinidad.* Berkeley: University of California Press.

Roseman, Marina. 1991. *Healing Sounds from the Malaysian Rainforest: Teimar Music and Medicine.* Berkeley: University of California Press.

Roubekas, Nickolas P. and Robert A. Segal, eds. 2017. *The Wiley Blackwell Companion to the Study of Religion.* Hoboken: Wiley-Blackwell.

Rouget, Gilbert. 1985. *Music and Trance: A Theory of the Relations between Music and Possession.* Brunhilde Biebuyck, trans. Chicago: University of Chicago Press.

Sahlins, Marshall. 2022. *The New Science of the Enchanted Universe: An Anthropology of Most of Humanity.* Princeton: Princeton University Press.

Sakakeeny, Matt. 2015. "Music." *Keywords in Sound.* David Novak and Matt Sakakeeny, eds. Durham, NC: Duke University Press, 112–124.

Sakata, Hiromi Lorraine. 1983. *Music in the Mind: The Concepts of Music and Musician in Afghanistan*. Kent, OH: Kent State University Press.

Sanga, Imani. 2013. "The Limits and Ambivalences of Postcolonial Consciousness in Mbunga's *Church Law and Bantu Music*." *Yearbook for Traditional Music* 45: 125–141.

Sawa, George Dimitri. 1985. "The Status and Roles of the Secular Musicians in the Kitāb al-Aghānī (Book of Songs) of Abu al-Faraj al-Iṣbahānī (D. 356 A. H./967 A. D.)." *Asian Music* 17(1): 69–82.

Schielke, Samuli. 2019. "The Power of God. Four Proposals for an Anthropological Engagement." *ZMO Programmatic Texts* 13. http://d-nb.info/1175974781/34

Schmidt, Leigh Eric. 2000. *Hearing Things: Religion, Illusion, and the American Enlightenment*. Cambridge, MA: Harvard University Press.

Schultz, Anna C. 2020. "Still an Ethnomusicologist (for Now)." *Journal of Musicology* 37(1): 39–50.

Schultz, Anna C. 2013. *Singing a Hindu Nation: Marathi Devotional Performance and Nationalism*. New York: Oxford University Press.

Seeger, Anthony. 1987. *Why Suyá Sing: A Musical Anthropology of an Amazonian People*. Cambridge: Cambridge University Press.

Şenay, Banu. 2020. *Musical Ethics and Islam: The Art of Playing the Ney*. Urbana: University of Illinois Press.

Shelemay, Kay Kaufman. 1989. *Music, Ritual, and Falasha History*. East Lansing: Michigan State University Press.

Shelley, Braxton D. 2023. *An Eternal Pitch: Bishop G. E. Patterson, Broadcast Religion, and the Afterlives of Ecstasy*. Berkeley: University of California Press.

Shelley, Braxton D. 2021. *Healing for the Soul: Richard Smallwood, the Vamp, and the Gospel Imagination*. New York: Oxford University Press.

Shelley, Braxton D. 2020. "'I Love It When You Play that Holy Ghost Chord': Sounding Sacramentality in the Black Gospel Tradition." *Religions* 11(9). https://doi.org/10.3390/rel11090452

Sherinian, Zoe C. 2014. *Tamil Folk Music as Dalit Liberation Theology*. Bloomington: Indiana University Press.

Shiloah, Amnon. 1995. *Music in the World of Islam: A Socio-Cultural Study*. Detroit: Wayne State University Press.

Silverstein, Michael. 1976. "Shifters, Linguistic Categories, and Cultural Description." *Meaning in Anthropology*. Keith Basso, ed. Albuquerque: University of New Mexico Press, 11–57.

Slobin, Mark. 1976. *Music in the Culture of Northern Afghanistan*. Tucson: Wenner-Gren Foundation.

Smart, Ninian. 1973. *The Science of Religion and the Sociology of Knowledge*. Princeton: Princeton University Press.

Smith, Johnathan Z. 1998. "Religion, Religions, Religious." *Critical Terms for Religious Studies*. Mark C. Taylor, ed. Chicago: University of Chicago Press, 269–284.

Southern, Eileen. 1997. *The Music of Black Americans: A History*, third edition. New York: Norton.

Southern, Eileen. 1977. "Musical Practices in Black Churches of Philadelphia and New York, ca. 1800–1844." *Journal of the American Musicological Society* 30(2): 296–312.

Spencer, Jon Michael (Yahya Jongintaba). 1991. *Theological Music: Introduction to Theomusicology*. New York: Greenwood Press.

Srinivas, Tulasi. 2018. *The Cow in the Elevator: An Anthropology of Wonder.* Durham, NC: Duke University Press.

Stausberg, Michael and Steven Engler, eds. 2022. *The Routledge Handbook of Research Methods in the Study of Religion.* New York: Routledge.

Stausberg, Michael and Steven Engler, eds. 2016. *The Oxford Handbook of the Study of Religion.* New York: Oxford University Press.

Steingo, Gavin and Jim Sykes, eds. 2019. *Remapping Sound Studies.* Durham, NC: Duke University Press.

Sterne, Jonathan. 2011. "The Theology of Sound: A Critique of Orality." *Canadian Journal of Communication* 36(2): 207–225.

Sterne, Jonathan. 2003. *The Audible Past: Cultural Origins of Sound Reproduction.* Durham, NC: Duke University Press.

Stokes, Martin. 2023. *Music and Citizenship.* New York: Oxford University Press.

Stokes, Martin. 2018. "Notes and Queries on 'Global Music History.'" *Studies on a Global History of Music: A Balzan Musicology Project.* Reinhard Strohm, ed. New York: Routledge, 3–17.

Stokes, Martin. 2002. "Silver Sounds in the Inner Citadel?: Reflections on Musicology and Islam." *Interpreting Islam.* Hastings S.C. Donnan, ed. London: Sage Publications, 167–189.

Stolow, Jeremy, ed. 2013. *Deus in Machina: Religion, Technology, and the Things in Between.* New York: Fordham University Press.

Stone, Robert. 2010. *Sacred Steel: Inside an African American Steel Guitar Tradition.* Urbana: University of Illinois Press.

Sullivan, Lawrence E., ed. 1997. *Enchanting Powers: Music in the World's Religions.* Cambridge, MA: Harvard Center for the Study of World Religions.

Summit, Jeffrey A. 2016a. *Singing God's Words: The Performance of Biblical Chant in Contemporary Judaism.* New York: Oxford University Press.

Summit, Jeffrey A. 2016b. "Technology and the Transmission of Oral Tradition in the Contemporary Jewish Community." *Resounding Transcendence: Transitions in Music, Ritual, and Religion.* Jeffers Engelhardt and Philip V. Bohlman, eds. New York: Oxford University Press, 147–162.

Summit, Jeffrey A. 2000. *The Lord's Song in a Strange Land: Music and Identity in Contemporary Jewish Worship.* New York: Oxford University Press.

Swijghuisen Reigersberg, Muriel and Brian Schrag (forthcoming). "Ethnodoxology." *The Oxford Handbook of Music and Christian Theology.* Steve Guthrie and Bennett Zon, eds. New York: Oxford University Press.

Sykes, Jim. 2020. "The Secularism of Music Studies." *Yale Journal of Music & Religion* 6(2): article 8. https://doi.org/10.17132/2377-231X.1210

Sykes, Jim. 2018. *The Musical Gift: Sonic Generosity in Post-War Sri Lanka.* New York: Oxford University Press.

Sykes, Jim. 2015. "Sound Studies, Religion and Urban Space: Tamil Music and the Ethical Life in Singapore." *Ethnomusicology Forum* 24(3): 380–413.

Taruskin, Richard. 2005. *The Oxford History of Western Music Volume 1: Music from the Earliest Notations to the Sixteenth Century.* New York: Oxford University Press.

Taylor, Charles. 2024. *Cosmic Connections: Poetry in the Age of Disenchantment.* Cambridge, MA: Harvard University Press.

Taylor, Charles. 2007. *A Secular Age.* Cambridge, MA: Harvard University Press.

Taylor, Mark C., ed. 1998. *Critical Terms for Religious Studies.* Chicago: University of Chicago Press.

Taylor, Timothy D. 2024. *Making Value: Music, Capital, and the Social.* Durham, NC: Duke University Press.

Tedlock, Barbara. 1991. "From Participant Observation to the Observation of Participation: The Emergence of Narrative Ethnography." *Journal of Anthropological Research* 47(1): 69–94.

Titon, Jeff Todd. 2021a. "Ethnography in the Study of Congregational Music." *Studying Congregational Music: Key Issues, Methods, and Theoretical Perspectives.* Andrew Mall, Jeffers Engelhardt, and Monique M. Ingalls, eds. New York: Routledge, 64–80.

Titon, Jeff Todd. 2021b. "The Expressive Culture of Sound Communication Among Humans and Other Beings: A Phenomenological Approach." *The Oxford Handbook of the Phenomenology of Music Cultures.* Harris M. Berger, Friedlind Riedel, and David VanderHamm, eds. New York: Oxford University Press, 102–134.

Titon, Jeff Todd. 2020. *Toward a Sound Ecology: New and Selected Essays.* Bloomington: Indiana University Press.

Titon, Jeff Todd. 2019. "Ecojustice, Religious Folklife, and a Sound Ecology." *Yale Journal of Music & Religion* 5(2). https://doi.org/10.17132/2377-231X.1142

Titon, Jeff Todd. 2018 [1988]. *Powerhouse for God: Speech, Chant, and Song in an Appalachian Baptist Church.* Knoxville: University of Tennessee Press.

Titon, Jeff Todd. 2015a. "Thoreau's Ear." *Sound Studies* 1(1): 144–154.

Titon, Jeff Todd. 2015b. "Why Thoreau?" *Current Directions in Ecomusicology: Music, Culture, Nature.* Aaron S. Allen and Kevin Dawe, eds. New York: Routledge, 69–80.

Titon, Jeff Todd. 2008. "Knowing Fieldwork." *Shadows in the Field: New Perspectives for Fieldwork in Ethnomusicology*, second edition. Gregory Barz and Timothy J. Cooley, eds. New York: Oxford University Press, 25–41.

Titon, Jeff Todd. 2006. "'Tuned Up with the Grace of God': Music and Experience Among Old Regular Baptists." *Music in American Religious Experience.* Philip V. Bohlman, Edith L. Blumhofer, and Maria M. Chow, eds. New York: Oxford University Press, 311–334.

Titon, Jeff Todd. 1996. "Preface." *Worlds of Music: An Introduction to the Music of the World's Peoples*, third edition. Jeff Todd Titon, ed. New York: Schirmer, xxi—xxiv.

Titon, Jeff Todd. 1995. "Bi-Musicality as Metaphor." *Journal of American Folklore* 108(429): 287–297.

Titon, Jeff Todd. 1991. "Reflexivity and the Study of Religious Folklife." Unpublished paper delivered at the Annual Meeting of the American Folklore Society.

Titon, Jeff Todd. 1985. "Stance, Role, and Identity in Fieldwork among Folk Baptists and Pentecostals." *American Music* 3(1): 16–24.

Titon, Jeff Todd. 1980. "A Song from the Holy Spirit." *Ethnomusicology* 24(2): 223–231.

Tlostanova, Madina. 2023. "Decoloniality: Between a Travelling Concept and a Relational Onto-Epistemic Politican Stance." *Coloniality and Decolonization in the Nordic Region.* Adrián Groglopo and Julia Suárez-Krabbe, eds. New York: Routledge, 145–163.

Trouillot, Michel-Rolph. 1995. *Silencing the Past: Power and the Production of History.* Boston: Beacon Press.

Tsing, Anna Lowenhaupt. 2015. *The Mushroom at the End of the World: On the Possibility of Life in Capitalist Ruins.* Princeton: Princeton University Press.

Tuck, Eve and K. Wayne Yang. 2014. "R-Words: Refusing Research." *Humanizing Research: Decolonizing Qualitative Inquiry with Youth and Communities.* Paris Django and Maisha T. Winn, eds. Thousand Oaks, CA: Sage Publications, 223–248.

Turino, Thomas. 2008. *Music as Social Life: The Politics of Participation.* Chicago: University of Chicago Press.

Turner, Tamara Dee. 2023. "Learning to Trance: The Affective Grounding of Becoming Another Body in Another Place." *Other Worlds, Other Bodies: Embodied Epistemologies and Ethnographies of Healing.* Emily Pierini, Alberto Groisman, and Diana Espírito Santo, eds. New York: Berghahn, 153–173.

Turner, Victor. 1969. *The Ritual Process: Structure and Anti-Structure.* Chicago: Aldine Publishing.

Tuzin, Donald. 1984. "Miraculous Voices: The Auditory Experience of Numinous Objects [and Comments and Replies]." *Current Anthropology* 25(5): 579–596.

van der Veer, Peter. 2014. *The Modern Spirit of Asia: The Spiritual and Secular in China and India.* Princeton: Princeton University Press.

Viveiros de Castro, Eduardo. 1998. "Cosmological Deixis and Amerindian Perspectivism." *The Journal of the Royal Anthropological Institute* 4(3): 469–488.

Wallace, Maurice O. 2022. *King's Vibrato: Modernism, Blackness, and the Sonic Life of Martin Luther King Jr.* Durham, NC: Duke University Press.

Wei, Li. 1992. "The Duality of the Sacred and the Secular in Chinese Buddhist Music: An Introduction." *Yearbook for Traditional Music* 24: 81–90.

Weiner, Isaac. 2014. *Religion Out Loud: Religious Sound, Public Space, and American Pluralism.* New York: New York University Press.

Weiss, Sarah. 2019. *Ritual Soundings: Women Performers & World Religions.* Urbana: University of Illinois Press.

Williams, Richard David. 2024. "Epistemological *Jugalbandī*: Sound, Science, and the Supernatural in Colonial North India." *Acoustics of Empire: Sound, Media, and Power in the Long Nineteenth Century.* Peter McMurray and Priyasha Mukhopadhyay, eds. New York: Oxford University Press, 134–155.

Williams, Richard David. 2022. "Singing in Tune with God: Bengali Vaiṣṇava Musical Scholarship in the Eighteenth Century." *South Asian History and Culture* 13(2): 180–196.

Williams, Richard David. 2020. "Sounding Out the Divine: Musical Practice as Theology in Samāj Gāyan." *The Oxford History of Hinduism: Hindu Practice.* Gavin Flood, ed. New York: Oxford University Press, 342–361.

Williams, Richard David. 2019. "Playing the Spinal Chord: Tantric Musicology and Bengali Songs in the Nineteenth Century." *Journal of Hindu Studies* 12(3): 319–338.

Witulski, Christopher. 2018. *The Gnawa Lions: Authenticity and Opportunity in Moroccan Ritual Music.* Bloomington: Indiana University Press.

Wolf, Richard K. 2014. *The Voice in the Drum: Music, Language, and Emotion in Islamicate South Asia.* Urbana: University of Illinois Press.

Wong, Deborah. 2001. *Sounding the Center: History and Aesthetics in Thai Buddhist Performance.* Chicago: University of Chicago Press.

Index

For the benefit of digital users, indexed terms that span two pages (e.g., 52–53) may, on occasion, appear on only one of those pages.

Figures are indicated by an italic *f* following the page number

'*adhān* 33*f*, 47–48, 53–54
aesthetics 40–41, 53, 65, 80–81, 92–94
  Romantic aesthetics xxivn.8, 10
agency 25–26, 29n.23, 30n.29
  of Father/Yahweh 3–5
  of God 3–5, 23–24, 25
  and the "God question" 72
  of the Holy Spirit xx–xxi, 86–87
  human 12–13
  of listeners/auditors 53, 57, 62–63
  of orichas 83
  other-than-human xvi–xix, xxivn.8, 12–15, 17–20, 27, 40–43, 69–70
  of sṭambēlī saints 92
Amherst College 97–99, 100–1
Amiot, Jean Joseph Marie 32–34
anhad 68, 93
antiracist praxis and futures xviii, xxii, 17, 22–23, 36, 94
audibile
  musically xix, xx–xxi, 9–10, 92–93, 100–1, 105–6
  sound 47, 66n.6, 80–81
audible/inaudible continuum xix, 101–2, 107n.14
audibility, religion's 103–4, 105
audition. *See also* samā'
  divine 16
  in Islam 53, 54, 57
Augustine 8–9
aurality 103–4, 106n.8
  in Islam 8

Bakhle, Janaki 74–75
Balinese gamelan. 76, 78
Barz, Gregory 64
bebuten trancing. *See* Balinese gamelan
Becker, Judith vii, 76–78, 87, 90–91, 96, 104
belief xvii–xviii, 18–20, 21, 24, 32, 40–41, 64, 66n.2, 77, 80
  belief-inclusive research 15
  vs. knowledge 19–20
  religion as xv–xvi, xvii–xviii, 19–20, 28n.4, 28n.11, 96, 106n.1
Berliner, Paul xvii–xviii, 50–51
Bernard, Jean Frédéric 17, 32–37, 44
bhakti 75, 96–97
Bhatkhande, Vishnu Narayan 74
Bialecki, Jon 70
binary/binaries 29n.17, 51–52, 106n.3
  religion/secular and secular/nonsecular 7, 25–26, 38, 41–42, 86–87
bi-musicality 27, 42
Black gospel
  episteme 83, 90–91
  Gospel Imagination 87, 89
  tradition 17, 68, 83
Blacking, John 12–14, 26, 47, 66–67n.12, 72–73
Bohlman, Philip 47–49, 64, 66n.7, 104
bracketing
  of other-than-human agency xvi–xvii, xviii–xix, xxii–xxiii, 17–20, 21, 22, 26, 40–41, 55–57, 94
  of religion xix–xx, 42, 105
Butler, Melvin 17–18, 20–22, 68–69, 90, 105

call-and-response 1–2, 3–5, 25–26, 27n.2, 58–59, 87–88

Campbell Brothers, The 97–100, 105–6
Campbell, Chuck 100–1, 105–6
Catholicism 5–6, 32, 34–36, 93–94
chama 1, 3–7, 25, 103–4
chant 43
  Diné 38–40
Christianity 32–34
  in anthropology and ethnomusicology 49, 66n.11
  Black 87
  and the secular xv–xvi
colonial, logics of religion 64
colonialism 20
coloniality 70–71
Cooley, Timothy 15
Cuba 79–82, 97

decolonial xix, xxivn.11
  ethnomusicology xv, xviii, xxii, 22–23
decolonization 70–71
  in ethnography 70
  in ethnomusicology 69, 96
deep listening 76
difference 22–23, 32
  culturalist xx–xxi, 91
  onto-epistemic xxii–xxiii, xxiiin.6, 16, 20, 40, 47–48, 100–1
  religion as xv–xvi, xvii, 5–6, 9–10, 15, 18–19, 41–42
  and "taking seriously" 70–72, 79–80, 94
  as unbelonging xx
Diné 38–42
(dis)entangled ethnomusicology xxii, 97, 99–101, 102, 106n.3
disentangling music and religion xv, xvii–xviii, xx–xxi, xxii–xxiii, 11–14, 17–23, 63–64, 68
  as culturalist 9, 11

ecstasy 47, 50, 51–52, 53, 62–63, 68, 78
Eleguá 81–83
Enemy Way (Ana'í Ndáá') 38–42
Enlightenment (European) xv–xvi, 32, 37, 49, 71–72
  and religion 10, 11
entangling music and religion xv, xviii, xxii, 11, 72–73, 105–6
epistemology 90–91, 96
  of faith 17–18, 22
  secular xv–xvi, 70–71
Estonia xx–xxi, 24
  Võru xx
ethics of style 23–24, 92–93
ethnography
  access and extraction xx
  crisis of 26
  as extraction xvi–xvii, xx
  "Godly" 30–31n.43, 69–70, 71–72
  musical 15
  nonsecular 69, 73–74, 93
  observant participation xvii, 20
  participant observation xvii, 15
  positionality xviii, xix, xxii, 13–15, 17–18, 22–23, 41–42, 57–58, 65–66, 68–69, 72, 76, 77, 79–81, 82, 83, 84, 86–87
  refusal xx–xxi, 6, 27
  as scientism xvi–xvii
ethnomusicology
  as anointed 9–10
  anthropological xvi–xvii
  and the audible xix, 105–6
  as colonial 27, 102
  culturalist xvi, xx–xxi, xxii, 11–12, 16–17, 18–19, 38, 41–42, 43, 62–63, 70–71, 94, 96
  development as a discipline 32, 36, 43, 53, 102
  epistemological limits 57, 58
  Eurological/non-Eurological xviii, xxi–xxii, 22–24, 29n.21, 72–73, 90–91, 94
  Europhone xv
  and extraction 13–14, 30–31n.43, 69
  Islamic 54
  musical xvi–xvii
  nonsecular xviii, 16, 20, 22–23, 26, 83, 87–88, 90, 100–1
  and refusal xx
  and religion 10, 48–49
  and renewal 90–91
  secular xviii, xxi–xxii, 9–10, 22, 26, 68, 100–1
  secular unconscious in xvi–xvii, 75
  theistic 79–80
  the theological in 68

Eurological thought 34–35, 36

faith xvii–xviii, 77, 87
  epistemology of 22
al Faruqi, Lois Ibsen 44–45, 47–48, 51, 55, 56*f*, 57
Friedson, Steven M. 91–92
functionalism/functionalist xvi–xvii, xviii–xix, 11–12, 13, 14–15, 25, 77
Furani, Khaled 70–71

al-Ghazālī, Abū Ḥāmid Muḥammad 8–9, 44–45, 53–54, 55–57
gender 6–7, 64–65, 76, 79–80, 81–82, 84–85, 86–87
Gerson-Kiwi, Edith 43, 44, 47–48, 51
Godly ethnography. *See* ethnography
Gospel Imagination. *See* Black gospel

habitus of listening 76–77, 87, 104
Hackett, Rosalind 15
Hagedorn, Katherine 79–83
ḥalāl 55
ḥarām 55
Harris, Rachel 64–65
Herndon, Marcia 13–14
Hindustani and Carnatic music 74
Holiness-Pentecostal worship 97–99, 100–1, 105–6
Holy Spirit xx–xxi, 17–19, 20, 21, 84–86, 98–99, 100–1
Hood, Mantle 27, 42
House of God (Holiness-Pentecostal) 97–98, 99, 100, 105–6, 106n.7

identity 19–20, 65, 66n.7, 106n.2
  music and identity episteme 49, 73
immediacy. *See* mediation
improvisation 3–5, 58–59
inaudible
  efficacy of music and sound 80–81, 92–93
  more-than-human xxivn.8
  other-than-human beings xvii–xviii, xix, 29n.22, 70
  powers of Orthodoxy xx
  religion as 101–2, 105–6
  sound and vibration xix, 47

invisible
  other-than-human beings xvii–xviii, 29n.22, 46, 70, 102–4
  subjects of belief 88
Islam 5–6, 10–11, 34–35
  Islamic anthropology and ethnomusicology 54, 95n.4
  Islamization 64–65
  legal status of music in 47–48, 53–54, 64–65 (*see also* samā' polemic)
  Uyghur 64–65
Islamic practice
  audition in 54–55, 57
  aurality in 8
  ontologies of voice, sound, and music 55

Jankowsky, Richard C. 68–69, 92
Jones, Alisha Lola 68–69, 83, 84–90

Kaur, Inderjit N. 68–69, 93
Kenya 1, 5
  Kayole, Nairobi 1–2
  Matopeni neighborhood 1–2, 3–5
Khusrau, Amir 58–59, 61
kīrtan 96–97, 106n.2
Kiswahili 1–2, 3–5
Kligman, Mark 65
knowledge
  divine xv–xvi, 80–81
  ethnographic xx, 57, 87
  nonsecular 80–81, 85, 96
  of other-than-human agents xvi–xvii, xviii–xix, 6, 9, 11, 13–14, 57, 72, 77, 85, 90–91, 103–4
  performed 42
  of practice xx–xxi, 22, 37, 42, 63, 68–69, 97
  prophetic 7
  rather than belief 19–20, 28n.11
  religious xvi, xix–xx, 86–87, 94
  secular xv–xvi, xvii–xviii, 9–10, 96
  Sufi 57–58
  theological 23–24, 68, 69

Luhrmann, Tanya M. 29n.22, 70, 76, 77, 90–91, 95n.7, 103

mahfil-e-samā' 58–59, 61, 62–63

Mahmood, Saba 71–72
mapambio 1–2, 3–5, 25–26
McAllester, David 22–23, 38–42, 100–1
McLeod, Norma 13–14
Meadows, Ruthie 97
media xix–xxiv, 26, 27, 42, 64–65, 66n.7, 101–2
mediation 6, 7, 14–15, 59, 101–2
  humans and 40–41, 42, 57
  and immediacy 81, 93
  and other-than-human agency 30n.29
  religion as 29n.22
Merriam, Alan 11–14, 42
metalanguage 87–88, 90, 100–1
methodology
  and decolonization 96
  disentangling as 64
  methodological agnosticism xvii–xviii, xix–xx, 13–14, 16, 17–18, 19, 20–21, 22, 24, 48–49, 57–58, 68, 76, 79–81, 90–91
  methodological atheism xvi, xix–xx, 12–14, 16, 17, 20–21, 40–41, 42, 44, 46, 47, 48–49, 68, 70
  methodological ludism 14–15, 48–49
  methodological theism xviii–xix, 14–15, 16, 17–18, 20, 22, 24, 68–69, 72, 79–80, 82, 83, 86–87, 90–91
  nonsecular 93
  secular xv–xvi
  and style analysis 44–45
modernity
  Jewish musical 64
  as secular xv–xvi
  as secularization xv–xvi
Moll, Yasmin 69–70, 71–72
Mt. Calvary Holy Church Christian Restoration Centre 1–2, 5–7, 25–26, 97, 103–4
music studies xxi–xxii, 5–7, 15, 16, 22–23, 29n.21, 30n.29, 30n.38, 49, 63–64, 73, 86–87, 94, 102, 105–6
musicandreligion *xv*, xix, 11, 26, 68, 90–91, 97
mystery
  and epistemology xxii, 58
  and human senses 45–46
  sonic 46

Needham, Rodney 43–44, 47–48, 51
Nettl, Bruno 14–15, 104

ontology
  and difference 16, 40, 47–48, 100–1
  flat 16, 20, 26, 46, 52, 70
  musical 11–13
  ontological turn xix
  relational 55–57, 68, 93
  and relativism 55
  sonic 10, 55, 80–81, 83, 90–91
oricha 51–52, 79–83, 97
òrìṣà. *See* oricha
orisha. *See* oricha
Orsi, Robert xxiiin.3, 30n.41, 94, 103
Orthodox Christianity xx–xxi, 5–6, 23–24
other-than-human. *See* agency, bracketing, inaudible, invisible, knowledge, *and* mediation

Paluskar, Vishnu Digambar 74–75
Pentecostal Christianity xx–xxi, 17–19, 20, 21, 76, 84–87, 97–101, 105–6
Picart, Bernard 17, 32, 34–35, 36, 37, 44
positionality. *See* ethnography
possession, ritual and performance 12–13, 21, 50, 51–52, 80, 82, 91, 92
Protestant Christianity xvii–xviii, xx–xxi, 5–6, 32, 34–35, 36, 64–65

Qawwali 57–63, 76
Qur'ān 8, 47–48, 53–54, 55, 64–65, 71–72
  recitation 44–45, 47–48, 53–54, 64–65
Qureshi, Regula Burckhardt 57–63

Rangda. *See* Balinese gamelan
Rasmussen, Anne 64–65
religion
  as audible (*see* audibility, religion's)
  as belief (*see* belief)
  as colonial 10–11, 28n.5, 32–34

and colonialism 28n.4
comparative xvii–xviii, 34–35, 36, 43
as concept and category xv–xvi, xviii–xix, 5–6, 11, 25–26, 28n.4, 43, 44–45, 47
as culturalist 11, 20, 26, 41–42
as difference xvii, 9–10, 18–19, 32, 91
as disentangled (*see* disentangling music and religion)
as entangled (*see* entangling music and religion)
and ethnomusicology 10–16, 47–49, 101–2
Eurological concept of 25–26
as inaudible (*see* inaudible)
invention of 5–6, 32
and secularity xv–xvi, xxivn.11, 5–6, 9–10, 11, 96–97
and trance (*see* trance)
world religions 17, 32–35, 37

ritual xv–xvi, xx, 6, 7, 13, 32, 37, 42, 43–44, 45–47, 49, 50, 51, 53, 58–59, 62, 63–65, 70, 76–77, 79–80, 81, 83, 91–92, 97
Robbins, Joel 72, 78, 87–88
Rommen, Timothy 92–93
Rouget, Gilbert 51–53

sacred musicologies xviii, 36, 37, 44–45, 68, 94
sacred steel gospel 97–101, 105–6
Sahlins, Marshall 94, 102
samā' 53, 55–58
samā' polemic 50, 53–55, 57, 58–59, 104
Santería 79–83
Schultz, Anna 96–97
secular xxiiin.3, 5–6, 17, 68–70, 74–75, 80–81, 85, 100–1
bias xvii–xviii
critique xviii–xix, xxi–xxii, 16
enchantment 30n.39, 75
enclosure 11
epistemes xvii, 9, 11, 51–52, 102
ethnomusicology's secular unconscious xvi–xvii, 69–71, 94
post-secular 22–23
reason xvi–xvii, 23–24
secularity xix, 9–10, 16, 19, 26, 70–71, 72–73
as colonial xv–xvi, 26
secularization xv–xvi, 32, 41–42
sexuality 22–23, 84–86
Shelley, Braxton 83, 87–90, 99, 105
Sherinian, Zoe 64–65
shout (gospel) 68, 88, 98–99, 100
Sikh 8–9, 68, 93
Sikhī 5–6, 93
Smallwood, Richard 84, 87, 89, 90
sonic theology 79–80, 105
sṭambēlī 92
structuralism/structure 43–44, 51–52, 55–58, 61, 62, 77, 84
Sufi/Sufism 53, 55–63, 68, 72–73, 76, 92
supernatural 13, 14–15, 40–41, 42, 45–46
Sykes, Jim 73, 75, 104

theology 68
and ethnography xvii, 70
and ethnomusicology xviii–xix, 18–19, 65–66, 72–73, 83
and methodology 24
musical theology 87
and secular scholarly traditions 40–41, 44
and sound (*see* sonic theology)
as theory 69–70, 72, 87–88, 90–91
theopolitics 86–87
Titon, Jeff Todd 17–20
trance/trancing 13, 21, 51–52, 76–78, 92
as culture 50, 52
and ecstasy 51–52
and healing 92
and other-than-human beings 52
"problem" of trance 50, 51–52, 57
and religion 76
Tuzin, Donald 45–48

unbelonging xix–xxii

universality 69, 96, 105–6
  of critical theory 23–24, 72
  of/in music 12–13, 43, 44–45, 47–49, 57
  of/in religion xv–xvi, 9–10, 32, 36–37, 43–45, 46, 47–48
  of/in trance 51–52, 77
unsound xix
voice 6–7, 22–23, 43, 53–54, 84–85, 99
  other-than-human xxiiin.2, 16, 46, 76, 104
  religious 47–48
  voicing 5

Witulski, Christopher 65